Divorce and Remarriage in the Church

Biblical Solution for Pastoral Realities

By
David Instone-Brewer

EasyRead Large

Copyright Page from the Original Book

InterVarsity Press
P.O. Box 1400, Downers Grove, IL 60515-1426
World Wide Web: www.ivpress.com
E-mail: email@ivpress.com

InterVarsity Press® is the book-publishing division of InterVarsity Christian Fellowship/USA®, a student movement active on campus at hundreds of universities, colleges and schools of nursing in the United States of America, and a member movement of the International Fellowship of Evangelical Students. For information about local and regional activities, write Public Relations Dept., InterVarsity Christian Fellowship/USA, 6400 Schroeder Rd., P.O. Box 7895, Madison, WI 53707-7895, or visit the IVCF website at <www.intervarsity.org>.

Unless otherwise indicated, all Scripture quotations are from The Holy Bible, English Standard Version, copyright © 2001 by Crossway Bibles, a division of Good News Publishers. Used by permission. All rights reserved.

Design: Cindy Kiple

Images: church: Elke Van de Velde/Getty Images
bride and groom: istockphoto.com

ISBN-10: 0-8308-3374-9
ISBN-13: 978-0-8308-3374-0

Printed in the United States of America ∞

Library of Congress Cataloging-in-Publication Data

Instone-Brewer, David.
  Divorce and remarriage in the church: biblical solutions for pastoral realities / David Instone-Brewer.
     p. cm.
  Includes bibliographical references.
   ISBN-13: 978-0-8308-3374-0 (pbk.: alk. paper)
   ISBN-10: 0-8308-3374-9 (pbk.: alk. paper)
   1. Divorce—Biblical teaching. 2. Remarriage—Biblical teaching.
 3. Divorce—Religious aspects—Christianity. 4. Remarriage—Religious aspects—Christianity. I. Title. BS680.D62I58 2006
241'.63—dc22
                                                          2006020863

P   19   18   17   16   15   14   13   12   11   10   9   8   7   6   5   4   3   2   1

Y   22   21   20   19   18   17   16   15   14   13   12   11   10   09   08   07   06

ReadHowYouWant partners with publishers to provide books for ALL Kinds of Readers. For more information about Becoming A **(RHYW)** Registered Reader and to find more titles in your preferred format, visit:

www.readhowyouwant.com

TABLE OF CONTENTS

"David Instone-Brewer is one of today's foremost scholars on first-century Judaism and its bearing on the New Testament. In this book he blends his academic expertise with pastoral concern; he sorts through most of the toughest issues with both intellectual rigor and Christian compassion. His persuasive work on this subject has already had far-reaching influence."

CRAIGS. KEENER, PROFESSOR OF NEW TESTAMENT, PALMER THEOLOGICAL SEMINARY, EASTERN UNIVERSITY

"Based on scholarly research, this book offers pastors, counselors and laypersons a coherent biblical understanding of divorce and remarriage. A valuable aspect of the book is that it can be read at several levels—discerning readers will appreciate the wealth of evidence that allows them to reach their own conclusions, while those interested in 'the bottom line' will find the author's summary principles on divorce and remarriage most helpful. A summary chapter gives helpful suggestions and questions especially useful for small group discussions. I look forward to using this most excellent book in my D.Min. family ministry class."

JACKB ALSWICK, PROFESSOR OF SOCIOLO-
GY AND FAMILY DEVELOPMENT, FULLER
THEOLOGICAL SEMINARY

"This is definitely the best and most compelling work I have read on the controversial
subject of divorce and remarriage. Dr. Instone-Brewer marshals evidence from rabbinic literature, the Dead Sea Scrolls and
other ancient texts to demonstrate the conclusion that the Bible permits (not 'commands' but 'permits') divorce on the grounds
of adultery (or sexual immorality of any
kind), neglect or abuse. Neglect includes desertion and the failure to provide food,
clothing and conjugal love. The author is also
very practical and helpful as he deals with
specific real-life cases. I highly recommend
this work."

KENNETH L. BARKER, FORMER SECRETARY
OF THE NIV COMMITTEE FOR BIBLE TRANS-
LATION

"With fresh insights from ancient sources,
Dr. David Instone-Brewer takes a deep yet
engaging look at this timely topic. He writes
with a scholar's mind and a pastor's heart.
Clergy, counselors and church councils should
read this book and then thoughtfully reflect

upon his conclusions regarding a biblical perspective on divorce and remarriage. People who are thinking about marriage, divorce and remarriage should also read this book as it offers both hope and challenge."

VIRGINIA TODD HOLEMAN, PROFESSOR OF COUNSELING, ASBURY THEOLOGICAL SEMINARY

"David Instone-Brewer knows the Scriptures, and the textual and cultural background to the Scriptures, as well as any biblical scholar in the world today. He combines this scholarship with a pastor's heart for people and a commitment to the church. Out of this powerful mix he has written an authoritative—perhaps *the* authoritative—treatment of divorce and remarriage in church life today. The crisp, breezy, accessible style of this book is a great strength. It is clearly written by a pastor for regular people. But underneath this accessibility is rock-solid scholarship. I think that *Divorce and Remarriage in the Church* will become an indispensable resource for both scholars and pastors in years to come, and has the promise of reforming church practices in thousands of congregations. I offer this book my highest endorsement."

DAVID P. GUSHEE, UNIVERSITY FELLOW AND GRAVES PROFESSOR OF MORAL PHILOSOPHY, UNION UNIVERSITY, AND AUTHOR OF *GETTING MARRIAGE RIGHT*

"The next time I teach or counsel on divorce and remarriage I'm heading straight for this book. Not only does it make the biblical texts clear, it makes it clear how to teach them."

DAVE HANSEN, KENWOOD BAPTIST CHURCH, CINCINNATI, OHIO

PREFACE

This book has been through several incarnations and has benefited from the input of many people, especially the congregation of Llanishen Baptist Church and my fellow minister Michael Ball, who all suffered several sermons on this subject while I was working through these ideas. My wife, Enid, has been equally long-suffering and has frequently steered me from theory to practical issues.

Most of the academic work that forms the foundation of this book has been published as papers in various scholarly journals and in my academic book on this topic, *Divorce and Remarriage in the Bible: The Social and Literary Context* (Eerdmans, 2002). I carried out most of this work as a research fellow at Tyndale House in Cambridge; I do not think it would have been possible to fully investigate all the varied aspects of the cultural background to the biblical text without the unequaled resources of Tyndale's superb library.

The readability of this book is due solely to Sheron Rice, who edited so diligently that she virtually rewrote the whole work and still managed to use most of my words. This book would not exist without her.

My aim in writing this book is to share insights that enabled me to understand the issue of divorce and remarriage through the eyes of the first readers of the New Testament. My hope is that the church will rediscover the biblical principles that divorce should occur only when marriage vows are broken and that only the wronged partner may decide whether this will happen. When people see that the church has practical and straightforward guidance to give on this subject, they may listen to its message that marriage should be life-long and that no one should divorce unless there are serious grounds for it.

INTRODUCTION

What's New?

"So what do you do for a living?" the young man asked me with a barely stifled yawn. He was trying to sell me a time-share apartment, and I was trying to get a free holiday without buying anything. I had to pretend to be interested in his product, and he had to pretend to be interested in me.

"I study the Bible at a research institute in Cambridge."

He looked up suspiciously, as though he had caught me lying: "I thought they'd have finished studying the Bible by now. What else is left for you to find out?"

I'd like to say that I took the opportunity to present the gospel to him, but I think I merely assured him that this was indeed what I did for a living and that there is lots of biblical research left to be done.

It's an unfortunate fact that there are still significant gaps in our knowledge of the language, culture and archaeology of the Bible. The first century especially has been less well understood because fewer non-biblical documents have survived than from surrounding centuries. At present, however, our knowledge of the first century is expanding rapidly, because we are beginning to properly understand the Dead Sea Scrolls and early rabbinic traditions as well as new scraps of ancient texts that are still being published.

The findings in this book are based on a multitude of new discoveries and academic publications by others and by me. The most important of these are as follows:

- Dead Sea Scroll fragments dealing with divorce, which help us to understand the other scrolls

- newly discovered Jewish divorce certificates, such as one written by a Jewish man on Masada in A.D.72 and one written by a Jewish woman in about A.D.125

- more than two hundred Aramaic, Greek and Latin marriage and divorce papyri, which have been collected together for the first time

- rabbinic evidence that can now be dated to the first century

- publication of hundreds of Samaritan documents, including ancient marriage contracts

- publication and analysis of all the rabbinic and Karaite marriage and divorce documents from the Geniza of the Cairo Synagogue

This wealth of new information gives us a much greater understanding of how people spoke and lived in the first century, and as a result we can read the New Testament with fresh insight. We are closer than ever before to understanding what it meant to its very first hearers and readers—and to understanding what God says to us today.

1

CONFESSIONS OF A CONFUSED MINISTER

Jesus never said, "What God has joined, no one can separate."

I was being interviewed for what would be my first church pastorate, and I was nervous and unsure what to expect. The twelve deacons sat in a row in front of me and took turns asking questions, which I answered as clearly as I could. All went reasonably smoothly, and then came the really tricky one: "What is your position on divorce and remarriage? Would you remarry a divorcee?"

I didn't know if this was a trick question or an honest one. There might have been a deep-seated pastoral need behind it, or it might have been a test of my orthodoxy. Either way, I didn't think I could summarize my view in one sentence; when I thought about it further, I couldn't decide what exactly my view was. I gave a deliberately vague reply: "Well, I guess it depends. Every case should be judged on its own merits."

It sounded good to me—and fortunately it must have sounded good to them, too, because they offered me the job—but I made a mental note to put a bit of study into the subject of divorce, quickly.

SO MANY QUESTIONS

It's a good thing I made that decision, because I soon needed a real answer to what had until then been merely a hypothetical question. My Baptist church was in a suburb with an Anglican and two Catholic churches nearby. Divorcees from these churches came to us asking if we would conduct their new wedding.

The Anglicans would say something along these lines: "Our vicar says we can't remarry in our church. He told us to get remarried at the courthouse and after that we could have a church blessing, but we want to say our vows before God, not to a civil registrar."

The Catholics had an additional problem: "My priest advised me to get my previous marriage annulled, but that would mean that it wasn't legally valid." One particularly upset man exclaimed, "I don't want to make my children into bastards!" Although Catholic theologians would say that isn't quite the way it works, it is how many people regard an annulment. All this made me very concerned that I find the right response to give to these sincere Christians.

Then I found that some of my deacons had been divorced and remarried. Should I throw them out of church leadership? If I did, I realized I'd be losing people who I believed to be some of the most spiritual in the church and who had exemplary Christian homes and marriages, which God appeared to have blessed.

I was surrounded by people who needed the right answer—but what *was* the right answer? I had always found the Bible passages about this to be confusing and contradictory.

- Why did Jesus sometimes say no to divorce and sometimes allow it?

- Why did Jesus allow divorce only for adultery while Paul allowed it only for desertion?

- Why was remarriage equivalent to adultery, even though it was after a divorce for adultery?

So I hit the books. Well, more specifically, one book—the Bible—and I was surprised by what I read. I wasn't surprised by the content, because I had read all the relevant passages many times before, but I was surprised because this time it suddenly made sense.

It had been some time since I'd last looked at these passages properly, and in the meantime I'd done a Ph.D. in first-century rabbinic Judaism. In the process I think I'd read everything the early Jews had written, so that this time, when I read the familiar New Testament texts again, I was doing so through the eyes of a first-century Jew—the people to whom Jesus and Paul had addressed their teaching. All the difficult texts on divorce and remarriage became clear.

Maybe not quite *all* the texts. I still had some questions to answer and some work to do. I didn't really understand the ancient Near Eastern context of Moses when he wrote down the laws of the Jews given to him by God at Mount Sinai, and I didn't understand all the Greek legal jargon in Paul's writings. I had to go and check a lot of Jewish documents again, but broadly speaking, the problems and contradictions that I had been used to seeing now became perfectly clear—and what's more, their teaching was sensible.

The trouble with most theologies of divorce is that they *aren't* sensible. They may give a reasonable account of most of the texts, in a forced way, but their conclusions just aren't practical in the fallen world we inhabit.

Most of society thinks that the Bible has nothing sensible to say about divorce and remarriage, and even many Christians think that they can ignore the Scriptures on this particular subject. The laws of Western nations, which are based largely on biblical principles, have deliberately avoided the issue of grounds for divorce by allowing no-fault divorce. This has resulted in a huge increase in divorces, as well as a feeling that marriage can be ended for just about any reason, and this in turn has resulted in disillusionment with the whole institution of marriage.

TRADITIONAL CHURCH TEACHING

People have interpreted what the Bible says about divorce and remarriage in two main ways (although there are many others):

1. There are two valid grounds for divorce, but remarriage is not allowed unless one of the former spouses has died.

2. There are no grounds for divorce or even for separation.

The first interpretation is the one given by most established churches. They conclude that Jesus and Paul both taught that there was one valid ground for divorce (although these were different). Jesus allowed the divorce of someone who had an adulterous partner, and Paul allowed the divorce of someone whose nonbelieving partner had deserted them. The interpretation goes on to say that neither Jesus nor Paul allowed remarriage unless one of the couple had died, because in some sense a marriage remains valid until it is ended by death. The main problem with this interpretation is that it is illogical: why do Jesus and Paul identify these two grounds for divorce but not allow divorce for physical abuse or other harmful situations?

The second main interpretation—which doesn't allow divorce for any reason—is more logical. It says that Jesus' ground of adultery applied only to the Jews of his day, because according to their laws, adultery led to compulsory divorce. It then says that Paul's ground of desertion by a non-Christian partner was, similarly, just for Romans of his day, because under Roman law desertion was equivalent to compulsory divorce. This interpretation tells modern believers that divorce is not allowed unless you are divorced against your will and that remarriage is not allowed unless you are widowed. Although this interpretation is more logical than the first, it is even less practical, because it means that someone can continue to commit adultery or physical abuse in the knowledge that their partner cannot end the marriage.

Other believers have decided that the Bible just isn't practical about these matters, so they have formulated their own "sensible" conclusion and tried to justify it according to Scripture. They say, for example, that divorce is allowed for adultery, abuse and abandonment committed by both nonbelieving and believing partners, and they base this teaching on principles they extrapolate from the text by sometimes dubious means. This type of interpretation comes out of a pastoral heart and a desire to help those who are in dreadful situations. While I commend and agree wholeheartedly with that desire, I believe it is far safer to arrive at a solution by looking at Scripture first and then following where it leads.

NO BLINDING FLASH

My sudden realization of how a first-century Jew would have understood these texts wasn't due to a blinding flash of inspiration but was the result of three years of hard work for my Ph.D., which suddenly came together: three years of reading huge sections of rabbinic literature, digging into the Mishnah, Tosefta Talmud, Midrashim, Philo and the Dead Sea Scrolls; analyzing the texts—especially to see how they interpret the Old Testament—and comparing my findings with those of medieval and modern scholars. At the end of all this I could think and interpret more like the ancient rabbis themselves, and I was able to unpack the highly abbreviated accounts of their debates.

When I reread the words of Jesus and Paul, I found details that would have been recognized by a contemporary rabbi but are meaningless to most modern readers. Both Jesus and Paul used the language and terminology used by the rabbis—especially when speaking about divorce, which was a hot topic of debate at that time. I suppose it's not surprising that they did so: Jesus was, after all, answering questions that were being posed by Pharisaic rabbis, and Paul said that he had been trained under

Gamaliel, who was a foremost rabbi of the time.

I suppose you think I'm now going to tell you what I discovered. Well, sorry, I'm not—just yet. It will take some time to explain, and until I've done so, the conclusions will have to wait. I will set it out in sections:

1. The Old Testament and God's divorce. Yes, God himself is a divorcee, and I was surprised to discover how strongly the Old Testament emphasizes this (chapters two to four).

2. Jesus' and Paul's teaching on divorce and remarriage (chapters five to seven).

3. How this teaching should work and a look at marriage vows (chapters eight to ten).

4. Church policy on divorce and remarriage, what churches should do now, and some e-mails about real-life problems (chapters eleven to fifteen).

"NO ONE CAN SEPARATE"?

But what I will tell you now is what I *didn't* find in the Bible. Just as Captain Kirk never said, "Beam me up, Scotty," and James Cagney never said, "You dirty rat," and Sherlock Holmes never said, "Elementary, my dear Watson," the Bible never says, "Those whom God has joined, no man can separate."

It's true that Jesus did say something very similar in Matthew 19:6, but his actual words (in a few representative translations) are these:

> What therefore God has joined together, let not man separate. (English Standard Version)

> What therefore God hath joined together, let not man put asunder. (King James Version)

> Therefore what God has joined together, let man not separate. (New International Version)

> No human being must separate, then, what God has joined together. (Good News Bible)

None of these translations of Jesus' words reads "no one can separate." Although the phrase "no one can separate" does not sound very different from "let no one separate" or "one must not separate," there is a world of difference in meaning.

If Jesus had said "no one *can* separate," it would mean that divorce is impossible, since once a couple has married, they will *always* be married in God's eyes. In other words, if God has joined a couple in marriage no one can "unjoin" them. This is an interesting idea, and although there are other hints in Scripture that may seem to back it up, we will see in chapter seven that they do not stand up to scrutiny. It is, in any case, something of a digression, because as I've said, the words "no one can separate" are not in Scripture.

The words that Jesus *did* say, "*let* no one separate," do not mean "it's not possible for you to separate"; they mean "it is possible to separate, but you should not."

To examine these words even further: when Jesus says "let no one separate," he is, in technical terms, using the imperative mood. Other possible meanings of the imperative are "should not" and "must not." Sometimes it can have a very strong sense of being an order ("don't!"), and at other times it can indicate a much weaker tone—"please don't do it!" But one thing the use of the imperative can *never* mean is "you cannot." The phrase can't be translated "it is impossible for you to separate" or "you are not able to separate" or "you cannot separate." What it actually means, therefore, is that separation is certainly possible but that it is wrong or, at the very least, undesirable.

So what does Jesus mean when he tells people not to separate? Clearly he is saying that it is wrong, but is he talking about divorce or about separation? The Greek word he uses for "separate"— *chōrizō*—is the word usually used to mean "divorce" (in fact, the standard lexicon for nonliterary Greek, Moulton & Milligan, even says that *chōrizō* was the technical term for "divorce"; although this is probably an exaggeration, it was certainly one of the technical terms for divorce). It's therefore clear that Jesus is making a plea or a command against *divorce* rather than separation. He isn't saying that divorce *cannot* happen but that it *shouldn't* happen.

And who is he saying this to? Who is the sinner in a divorce? Is it the person who decides to separate and starts the legal proceedings? Or is it the person who causes the divorce?

LOOKING FORWARD

We will see in later chapters that what defines a broken marriage is broken vows: the vows that marriage partners make to each other in God's presence. We will find in chapter three that the Old Testament describes God's relationship with Israel like a marriage that ended in divorce because of Israel's adulteries. So God is a divorcee—and he hates it as much as any victim of divorce.

A victim? Yes, God is a victim of divorce, even though he actually carried it out; in the same way, many victims today are actually the ones who initiate proceedings to bring the marriage to an official end. They call in the lawyers to stop the mockery and pain of constant adultery or the anguish of abuse. But as we will see, the Bible does not regard the victim as the sinner. It is the person who is guilty of causing the marriage to break up whom Jesus addresses when he says, "Those whom God has joined, no one should separate."

In other words, his warning is not to the person who finally tidies up the legal mess after the marriage has broken down but to those who would violate their marriage vows and, in so doing, cause the marriage to break up.

Jesus says that divorce should never happen because when two people marry they are joined by God, who is a witness to the marriage vows and is there to bless the marriage. These vows should never be broken—especially since they are made before God. But of course people do break them, just as they break God's other commands. Jesus never says that these vows are impossible to break—as if God ignores the reality of sin—but he teaches that if a partner breaks the vows and is then repentant, we should forgive that person. If the vows are continuously broken, without repentance, then the marriage will be left in shreds. Therefore although the breakup of a marriage is always due to sin, it is not the divorce itself that is the sin; the sin is the breaking of the vows, which causes the divorce.

In later chapters we will look at the biblical marriage vows closely. We will learn that the Bible allows only the victim to initiate a divorce—that is, it allows them to decide when enough is enough and, if their partner remains unrepentant, to decide that the marriage is over. Jesus' main complaint was that the Jews had abandoned this principle. They allowed a man to divorce his wife even when she hadn't broken her vows—that is, when he had no grounds for divorce. Paul similarly condemned a Greco-Roman groundless divorce.

Later on in the book we will look at the Old Testament's teaching on divorce and remarriage—which allowed divorce on the grounds of neglect or abuse—and discover that Jesus and Paul both affirmed this teaching.

PUTTING IT IN CONTEXT

This is all very different from what the church has been teaching for many, many years, and that, I agree, makes my conclusions rather suspect. There is a good reason, however, for the church to have misunderstood this teaching: our knowledge of first-century A.D. language and culture was lost, and critical facts about Jewish divorce had gone missing by the second century.

As all good preachers know, "a text without a context is a pretext," and this is a very important principle to remember if we are to understand the divorce issue. We need to know the cultural context of our texts in order to understand them. For example, we now know the reason Paul insisted that women covered their heads in church. At that time it was highly immodest for women to go bareheaded outside their own home; only prostitutes did so. Further, in the Corinthian society morals were under constant threat, and this made things especially difficult for the newly emerging church. Our modern-day church, for the most part, doesn't demand that women wear hats to church, although of course it's understandable that some people still want to keep to this teaching.

I will examine the cultural context in greater detail in later chapters and explain how we can discover what Jesus really taught about divorce. The implications of his teaching will be far more serious than the wearing of hats in church, however, and understandably many people will be reluctant to accept them.

What we have found out already is very important. We have discovered that the Bible may not say what we thought it did. Sometimes we come to the Bible already very sure about what it means, and this can keep us from reading it with the Spirit's guidance. Sometimes it's necessary to let ourselves forget what we think we know and read it afresh. That's what I had the chance to do as a young minister, and I had some extra help—some insight into how the rabbis thought.

God has given us Scripture, which is a book of personal experiences. It is full of histories, letters, prophetic messages and praise songs. It contains almost no theology, so we are left to work out the principles for ourselves—and we won't always come to the same answers. We are gradually leaving behind misunderstandings like the inherent sinfulness of sexual contact or the belief that there is no forgiveness for sins after baptism, though almost all the early church fathers adhered to these teachings. And we no longer burn heretics—which is fortunate for me, because some of you will conclude that I am one!

DRAW YOUR OWN CONCLUSIONS

My only aim in studying this topic and in writing this book has been to listen to God as he speaks to us through the Bible, and I hope that you are prepared to read the Bible again with me as I explain further. But please don't just accept what I say as being the correct interpretation. I'm not claiming any revelation from God, and many Christians interpret the texts in other ways. Paul says in 1 Corinthians

14:29 that we should judge the prophets, and if we are asked to judge those who bring direct revelations, then we should certainly also judge our Bible teachers. My prayer for readers of this book is that we will use Scripture, the help of the Holy Spirit and our intelligence to judge where the truth lies and then live by our conscience.

FURTHER READING

Traditional Church Teaching on Divorce

Deasley, Alex R.G. *Marriage and Divorce in the Bible and the Church.* Kansas City, Mo.: Beacon Hill, 2000. An excellent review of the church fathers' teachings on these subjects.

Heth, William A., and Gordon J. Wenham. *Jesus and Divorce.* London: Hodder & Stoughton, 1984. Chapters 1 and 2 provide a good survey but tend to ignore dissent among the church fathers.

Instone-Brewer, David. *Divorce and Remarriage in the Bible.* Grand Rapids: Eerdmans, 2002. Chapter 9, "History of Divorce," covers the church fathers, the Reformers and the positions of various modern churches.

Modern "Solutions" to New Testament Divorce Teaching

Adams, Jay E. *Marriage, Divorce and Remarriage in the Bible.* Phillipsburg, N.J.: Presbyterian & Reformed, 1980. Argues that abuse and neglect are un-Christian, so a believer can be divorced in response to them.

Atkinson, David. *To Have and to Hold: The Marriage Covenant and the Discipline of Divorce.* London: Collins, 1979. Argues that abuse and neglect break the seventh commandment.

Clark, Stephen. *Putting Asunder: Divorce and Remarriage in Biblical and Pastoral Perspective.* Brigend, U.K.: Brynterion, 1999. Takes the position that abuse and neglect show that the person is an unbeliever and does not want to remain married, so the believer can divorce that person.

Instone-Brewer, David. *Divorce and Remarriage in the Bible.* Grand Rapids: Eerdmans, 2002. Chapter 10, "Modern Reinterpretations," summarizes the huge variety of modern reinterpretations of the Bible texts.

2

A MARRIAGE MADE IN PARADISE

Moses' certificate of divorce.

Have you heard the one about Adam and his "spare rib"? Well, as you know, in the beginning God made Adam and put him in paradise. Adam was allowed to enjoy all the many wonders of the Garden of Eden and was given the job of naming all the animals. But after he had named them—rather a long task—he got bored. He wanted some company, someone he could talk to and impress.

God understood the situation perfectly. "I can see that you're lonely," he said to Adam. "Let me make a woman for you."

"What's a woman?" asked Adam.

"A woman will love and adore you. She'll cook perfect meals and always look nice. She'll laugh at all your jokes and she'll never complain."

"That's wonderful!" said Adam with enthusiasm. "But—she sounds very expensive. What will she cost me?"

"Ah," replied God, "a woman like that will cost you an arm and a leg."

Adam considered this carefully for a moment, then turned back to his Maker. "What will I get for one rib?"

GOD'S PERFECT PLAN

OK, so men aren't perfect either—and we certainly don't live in paradise anymore. Are we asking the impossible of marriage? Can we really live happily with each other's imperfections and strange, annoying habits—let alone our tendency toward downright selfishness? Even if we start off feeling that our partner can do no wrong, doesn't that phrase "the honeymoon period" sum up the truth that the blissful period of perfect love and contentment is but a short stage quickly passed through? The truth is that marriage is hard work—and many are often far from successful.

Marriages started to fail with Adam and Eve. When they were thrown out of paradise because of their disobedience, they soon encountered difficulties. And their reduced circum-stances were the least of their problems, for they themselves had changed—for the worse. They had both discovered the difference be-tween good and evil, and at the heart of this discovery was the desire to do what they wanted. This wasn't necessarily what God or the other person wanted, and it immediately led to conflict.

Like many couples, they found that having children didn't bring them closer together. It's hard enough for two people to want the same thing at the same time, but when there are three or four people in the family it becomes more and more difficult for them all to agree, especially when the children start growing into independent adults. Family gatherings, such as mealtimes, often become battlegrounds.

One admittedly tongue-in-cheek definition of the family is "a group of individuals who are united by a common TV set." As a family in-creases and starts to fragment, the number of TVs it owns also increases. To take the analogy back to early times, a family could be identified as a group that sat around the same campfire; when members of the family started to sit at different fires, relationships had clearly gone seriously wrong. It wasn't long before Adam's camp had a whole constellation of fires!

God is realistic about the problems of individuals living together, and from the beginning he had a plan designed to help couples stay together, a plan that goes some way to dealing with our quarrelsome individualism.

> Therefore a man shall leave his father and his mother and hold fast to his wife, and they shall become one flesh. (Gen 2:24)

In other words, God says, "When a couple get married they must leave their parents' home and set up a new home of their own." This sounds like very simple advice, but it is effective and in fact was quite countercultural for people of Old Testament times. Two adults have more than enough trouble living together happily without twenty-four hours a day of "helpful comments" from their parents.

There's a second part to God's instructions, and the first part works only if we follow this as well: "When you get married, whatever happens, stick together as though you were one person."

If the advice is followed, a man and woman will get married and commit themselves to each other totally. They will promise to stay together and try to act like one person. God tells them to leave both their family homes and make a new home—and he makes sure that no one else joins them for at least nine months. When the new person does arrive, he or she will only gradually develop an independent will, so that the couple has time to get used to having another individual living alongside them, with differing needs and expectations.

Children soon become individuals, of course. They quickly find out how to say "No!" when they don't want to do something. They learn how to argue, and then as teenagers they begin to think seriously and may reject a lot of what their parents tell them. It's not too long before they start to notice the opposite sex, and then before the parents know it, they have found someone they want to marry. After a painfully expensive though joyous wedding, things get better. The newlyweds leave Mom and Dad to set up home together, and the conflicts and frustrations experienced between parent and child are resolved. They find that their parents can be friends and confidants rather than oppressive tyrants, and God's wisdom is proved once more.

BUT IN PRACTICE...

Well, that's the theory, but more often than not it seems that marriages go wrong. Children stay at home longer now, mainly because education takes longer. Couples don't always start out having a home just to themselves for even nine months. And they don't always learn how to accommodate each other, let alone their children. They end up battling with each other and their children rather than communicating and negotiating. Sadly, but all too commonly, people stop trying to resolve their differences and give up on their relationship instead. Children run away, or, more often, one of the parents walks out. Often one parent has left long before the teenage battles with the children start, because they couldn't learn to live with their partner.

THE CRUEL WORLD OF THE ANCIENT NEAR EAST

The state of marriage today is certainly not healthy, but we would be wrong to assume that marriage problems are just a modern disease. Some of the most ancient laws open our eyes to historical problems within marriages.

King Hammurabi (who ruled ancient Babylon in 1800B.C.) is best remembered for his 282 laws carved on an eight-foot-high stone monument. To our minds, some of these laws were rather brutal—for example:

> King Hammurabi's Law Number 21: If one citizen tunnels through the wall of another's house and robs it, then the citizen is sentenced to death. The execution shall take place outside the tunnel and the body shall be used to fill the tunnel.

Nonetheless, these laws did mark the beginning of impartial justice. Instead of relying on the arbitrary decision of a ruler or a judge, everyone knew what punishment would be meted out for each crime, and they also knew what was and wasn't a crime.[1]

This system of laws solved many social problems—assigning punishments for criminals and compensation for victims—but they still left a host of difficulties and even created some new ones. For example, the system didn't help abandoned women, for a man was still allowed to walk out on his wife and children at any time without having to leave her any money or property or pay her any maintenance. In fact the law actually made things worse for her than before: it said that if her husband came back he could reclaim her and the children. The Middle Assyrian law (from 1400B.C.) was a little more humane than all the other laws of the ancient Near East, in that it did allow an abandoned wife to be free after five years.[2]

Imagine that you are a wife in the time of Moses or before. Your husband goes off with some friends to a market in another town, and his friends return without him. They report that he has fallen for a pretty young woman. Later they bring you a message from him: he isn't coming back, but you can keep the children and stay in the house he built—and good luck! This isn't very comforting, and it's only the beginning of your nightmare. If you don't find work, your family will soon starve and freeze. If you have enough land around the house for crops and sheep, it's possible to grow food, spin wool and barter for other goods, but all this is very hard work, especially for a single mother.

Unless you have grown sons who are strong enough to work the land (without the help of tractors and weed killer), you have very few choices. There are few professions for women, so either you have to go back to your parents' home (if they are still alive) or you have to get married again so that your new husband can work the land and teach your sons. It's very difficult, however, for you to get remarried when the law says that your original husband can reclaim you at any time and can also reclaim your children. He might wait till your children have become economically useful workers and then decide to enforce his rights. This means that your new husband would lose you and his stepchildren, whom he'd spent several years supporting, feeding and training. Any man who married you would have to accept this as a very real possibility, and so your chances of finding a new husband are very small.

MOSES MAKES THINGS BETTER

The one place where the law was fairer for abandoned women was Israel. The Ten Commandments came with many other laws that amplified these ten basic rules. This new code was a remarkable one and was more enlightened than any others in the ancient Near East.

For example, in Hammurabi's code, people were not considered equal. If you hurt an ordinary person you had to pay a fine, but if the person was "important," you were punished by being given equal injury.[3] According to the laws given to Moses, however, if you injured someone it didn't matter what their rank was. Whoever it was, you were punished by being given the same injury you had given to them—"eye for eye, tooth for tooth" (Ex 21:24). This was same punishment that was given under Hammurabi's law for harming a high-ranking official. In other words, everyone in Israel was treated with equal respect—and they were all treated as though they were important. (For the modern reader, of course, this level of punishment seems barbaric, but it was appropriate for the time—especially when compared with punishments in surrounding nations, which were often extremely gruesome.[4])

The most impressive differences between the laws of Israel and those of other ancient Near Eastern nations were in the laws of remarriage. In other countries it was difficult for an abandoned woman to get remarried, but in Israel this unfairness was corrected by giving her the right to receive a divorce certificate from her husband: "He writes her a certificate of divorce and puts it in her hand and sends her out of his house" (Deut 24:1).

This certificate had to be given to any woman who was abandoned or thrown out by her husband. It confirmed that her husband had divorced her and meant that it was safe for another man to marry her; he didn't have to worry that her first husband would return one day to demand his wife back.

EQUALITY UNDER THE LAW OF MOSES

In fact, Israelite women were not the only women in the ancient Near East to be given the right to receive such a certificate. Some privileged wives of high-ranking army officers were given a similar certificate if their husbands were missing and presumed dead after a battle. Without a body it was uncertain if the husband was really dead, and so the wife was not able to remarry, no matter how long he was missing. But the Middle Assyrian law made a special concession for such a wife: after waiting for two years without news of her husband, she was given a "certificate of widowhood." This contained the words "You are now free to marry any man you wish." These same words are found in all the Jewish divorce certificates that have survived from the earliest times, and we can therefore presume that these certificates were patterned on something like this ancient concession for war widows of high-ranking officers.[5]

All Israelites shared an equal rank in Moses' law; it wasn't just high-ranking women who could have this type of certificate but any woman whose husband abandoned her. The law of Moses recognized that our sinfulness can end a marriage, and it made sure that women didn't suffer more than could be avoided. I also imagine that the process of writing out a divorce certificate made a lot of men think again and possibly stopped them from making the wrong decision.

The fact that Israelite women could be given a divorce certificate doesn't mean that God thinks divorce is a good idea. He designed marriage to last forever—for both the couple's and the children's benefit—and the breakup of a marriage is always a disaster. We have learned, though, that we have to distinguish between marriage breakup, which is always wrong, and divorce, which is the legal recognition that a marriage has broken up. Moses' law did not say that it was acceptable to break up a marriage;

it merely prescribed the legal process that was necessary after a breakup had happened. It said that the man couldn't have his cake and eat it; he couldn't abandon his wife and expect her to be waiting for him at a later date. Whatever sin causes the marriage to break up, there should be a clean end. Neither partner should hold the other as a prisoner in a marriage that is dead.

ARE MARRIAGES ANY BETTER TODAY?

At first glance, the New Testament teaching on divorce is very different from the Old Testament teaching. In later chapters we will find that this is not quite the case. If it *were* very different, it would suggest that marriage or humanity had changed, so that we needed different laws.

Unfortunately the world has not changed much with regard to marriage, because just as many marriages break down now as in biblical times. The true extent of marriage breakup in the modern world was not recognized until the divorce laws were liberalized. Although easier divorce means that some people get divorced unnecessarily, no one divorces when they are happily married. The New Testament world and the modern world have just as many instances of broken marriage vows, because they both suffer the same human sinfulness as in the ancient Near East.

In the Roman Empire of New Testament times, divorce was very common. People married when they were young, and as the years went by, they were likely to feel differently about each other. It was easy to get divorced, and the law did nothing to discourage it. One partner could just walk out on a marriage without any need to divide up the property or provide maintenance for the children. Things are a little different today, as compulsory financial arrangements help to support the partner who brings up the children, but our society is becoming more and more similar to the Roman society of the first century: fewer couples are getting married, which means that either partner can simply walk out of the relationship, just as a spouse could walk out of their relationship under Roman law.

CONCLUSION: GOD'S LAW IN AN IMPERFECT WORLD

The world that God made, including marriage, was perfect and wonderful, but everything was spoiled when we rebelled and became selfish. God told Adam and Eve that, as a result of their sin, growing food would become difficult and there would be problems in the relationships between men and women (Gen 3:16-19). Many harvests failed, and many marriages too. When marriages failed, the woman, being more vulnerable, usually suffered most. The law of Moses limited the damage that divorce inflicts by forcing a divorcing man to give his ex-wife a certificate that would allow her to remarry.

In the next chapter, we will see that the laws of the Old Testament have even more to say on the subject of a broken marriage and that they are always on the side of the victim, whether it is the man or the woman.

FURTHER READING

Origin and Wording of the Jewish Divorce Certificate

Instone-Brewer, David. "Deuteronomy 24:1-4 and the Origin of the Jewish Divorce Certificate." *Journal of Jewish Studies* 49 (1998):230-43. This article provides some detailed analysis.

_____. *Divorce and Remarriage in the Bible.* Grand Rapids: Eerdmans, 2002. The middle of chapter 2, "The Pentateuch," summarizes most of the data.

Ancient Near Eastern Law Codes and the Old Testament

Instone-Brewer, David. *Divorce and Remarriage in the Bible.* Grand Rapids: Eerdmans, 2002. Chapter 2, "The Pentateuch," compares the law of Moses with other ancient Near Eastern law codes.

Matthews, Victor H., and Don. C. Benjamin. *Old Testament Parallels: Laws and Stories from the Ancient Near East.* New York: Paulist, 1997. Selects the most important examples and gives short introductions.

Pritchard, James B., ed. *Ancient Near Eastern Texts Relating to the Old Testament.* Princeton, N.J.: Princeton University Press, 1992. *ANET* contains virtually all the texts, except for a few recent discoveries.

The Modern Situation and How We Got Here

Forster, Greg. "The Changing Face of Marriage and Divorce." *Anvil* 17 (2000):167-78. Gives a quick review of all the relevant statistics for the United Kingdom.

The National Center for Health Statistics publishes the official record of marriages and divorces in the United States at <www.cdc.go v/nchs/products/pubs/pubd/nvsr/nvsr.htm.>

Stone, Lawrence. *Road to Divorce, England, 1530-1987.* Oxford: Oxford University Press, 1990. This highly academic book is made easy to read by a multitude of real-life stories from the past.

3

GOD THE RELUCTANT DIVORCEE

God's marriage contract and the grounds for his divorce from Israel.

The following is *not* a true story! A man—let's call him Fred—went to a cheese and wine function, where he was cornered by a church minister wearing a very tall clerical collar. Nervous, Fred mumbled to the minister that he wasn't really a religious person. Unfortunately this appeared to make the minister even more interested in him, so Fred was relieved when they were interrupted by a woman with a tray of drinks. Gratefully, Fred took a glass, but then the minister sniffed the tray suspiciously and said to the lady in an embarrassingly loud voice: "I would rather commit adultery than drink alcohol!"

Poor Fred, realizing that he had done something wrong but not sure what it was, put his drink back on the tray and said, "I'm very sorry—I didn't know there was a choice."

We can laugh at this because adultery is such a normal part of modern life. We are aghast when some countries punish adultery with imprisonment or even the death penalty. In the ancient Near East, however, adultery was always a capital offense, and often the husband was expected to carry out the punishment. Even suspected adultery resulted in a trial by ordeal in the temple. The woman had to drink a special mixture that supposedly harmed only the guilty (see the details in Num 5). In much of the ancient world, adultery was regarded as seriously as murder. Although today we may not put adultery in the same bracket as murder, it can certainly kill a marriage.

"THOU SHALT NOT COMMIT ADULTERY"

Under Old Testament law, if someone was found to have committed adultery, the punishment was not always the death penalty, but it did result in the death of a marriage: "When a man takes a wife and marries her, if then she finds no favor in his eyes because he has found some indecency in her ... he writes her a certificate of divorce and puts it in her hand and sends her out of his house" (Deut 24:1). The words "some indecency" in this text could be more literally translated "a thing of nakedness" or "a cause of sexual immorality,"[1] and they most likely refer to adultery. Some say that this sexual immorality could not have been adultery, because adulterers were killed (Lev 20:10); however, the death penalty was not always carried out, since Old Testament law was not applied uniformly throughout its history. This is God's lovingly realistic way of dealing with the consequences of human sinfulness: the victim of adultery should have the choice of whether to end the marriage or not.

Adultery is not, of course, the only sin that can end a marriage. Many marriages are killed by neglect or abuse. Christians today accept that the Bible allows divorce for adultery, but many believe that it does not allow divorce for reasons such as physical or emotional abuse, or when a man withholds money from his wife, or stops her going out, or when a wife neglects the children and leaves them filthy and starving. This has led Christians to feel confused and concerned, because they conclude that God isn't interested in such things, that these issues don't seem to touch his heart. But why? Why is adultery more valid a reason for divorce than cruelty? Why *wouldn't* God allow divorce in these situations? And why wouldn't a victim be allowed at the very least the choice of leaving such a marriage?

THREE MORE BIBLICAL GROUNDS FOR DIVORCE

In fact, the Bible *does* have a law that addresses this situation. Exodus 21:10-11 is a text that is usually forgotten, but it provides precisely what is needed, for it allows the victim of abuse or neglect to be freed from the marriage.

This text is actually a law about a slave who has married her master; it states the rights that she has if he decides to marry a second wife. This law tells him to make sure that he doesn't neglect his first wife when he marries a second:

> If he takes another wife to himself, he shall not diminish her food, her clothing, or her conjugal love. And if he does not do these three things for her, she shall go out for nothing, without payment of money. (Ex 21:10-11)[2]

At first glance this text doesn't seem to apply to us at all, since we don't have polygamy and we don't marry slaves (though in some marriages it may seem like it!). But we will see that it actually applies to all marriages.

Polygamy was allowed in the Old Testament, and human nature being what it is, when a man took a second wife he often neglected his first wife and favored the new one. This was especially likely if his first wife had been a slave before he married her. So the point of this law was to ensure that the first wife was treated fairly. It says that the husband would not be permitted to withhold food, clothing or conjugal love from her. If he did neglect any of these, she would be able to go free—that is, she could get divorced.

Before we dismiss this as irrelevant to our marriages today, it is important to remember that this is case law, not statute law, which means that the principles are more important than the details. Then as now, some laws were written as "statutes," summarizing a whole subject area (such as divorce), while other laws were "case law." Case law is a collection of decisions made by judges in actual cases that established a new legal principle. These rulings can then be applied to other cases that share something in common with the case that established the principle. For example, the statute law on keeping the sabbath is part of the Ten Commandments (Ex 20:8-11), but it does not define the punishment for breaking it.

When a man was caught gathering sticks on a sabbath (Num 15:32-36), his case was brought before Moses, who decided that he deserved death. This story, with the decision about the punishment, became an item of case law—the principle derived from it is that breaking the sabbath law makes one liable to the death penalty.

Exodus 21:10-11 is case law, so we have to ignore the details about slavery and polygamy and look for the *principles* that apply to all marriages that involve neglect. The rabbis found the following principles in this text, and I think they were right. They reasoned that if a slave wife had the right to divorce a husband who neglected to supply food, clothing and conjugal love, then a *free* wife would certainly also have this right. And they argued that if one of two wives had this right, so did an only wife. Furthermore, if a wife had these rights, then a husband was also entitled to divorce a wife who neglected him. The biblical principle that is established, therefore, is the right of someone to divorce their partner if they neglect their vow to provide food, clothing or conjugal love.

FOUR MARRIAGE VOWS

This means that the Old Testament recognizes four grounds for divorce. The first three are neglecting to provide food, clothing and conjugal love (by either husband or wife), and the fourth is committing adultery.

These four obligations parallel the vows exchanged by couples in Jewish marriages. They promised to feed, clothe, exchange conjugal love with and be faithful to each other. The man agreed to provide food and clothing, the woman agreed to cook and sew, and they both agreed to share conjugal love and be faithful.

Actually, technically only a wife could be divorced for adultery, because a man could have more than one wife. This did not make it OK for him to commit adultery, but it meant that he could not be divorced for doing so, because he had not promised sexual fidelity to his wife alone. Well, that's how some rabbis argued, but I am not sure I agree. They also said that Deuteronomy 24:1 speaks only about adultery by a woman, but Deuteronomy 24:1-4 is another example of case law, in which principles are more important than the details, and the principle is that adultery is a ground for divorce. Jesus put an end to this loophole by teaching monogamy, so that adultery became an equal ground for divorce for both sexes—but I will leave the teaching of Jesus for another chapter.

Thus the Old Testament provided very sensible laws about divorce. Each partner had to keep his or her four marriage vows to feed, clothe, share conjugal love and be faithful. The principles behind these vows were that they had to supply material support (food and clothing) and physical affection (conjugal love). Abusive situations were covered by these laws, because physical abuse and emotional abuse are extreme forms of neglecting material support and physical affection.

The only person who could choose to enact a divorce was the victim. If your partner broke his or her marriage vows, you could chose to divorce them, or you could choose to forgive them and try to salvage the marriage. You could not divorce a partner simply because you wanted to. (This had changed by the time of Jesus, as we will see later.)

GOD'S DIVORCE

These four biblical grounds for divorce are illustrated by God's marriage to Israel, which ended unhappily in divorce when Israel sinned. Many of the Old Testament prophets speak about the problems in that relationship.

Hosea was told to marry a prostitute, who continued to be unfaithful to him, in order to illustrate God's marriage to Israel (Hos 1-3). Ezekiel described how Israel committed adultery with other gods along with other sins that led to the divorce (Ezek 16; 23). Jeremiah warned Israel's sister nation Judah to watch out because she was heading the same way (Jer 3-4). Isaiah brought the good news that unlike Israel, who was divorced, Judah had only suffered separation and that God wished for reconciliation (Is 50).

Thus the Old Testament prophets describe God as a divorcee, and when you put together all the references, you find a clear and unanimous picture. God had married Israel at Mount Sinai in the wilderness, then brought his bride across the threshold of the Jordan into Palestine. There he gave her food (milk and honey) and wool for clothes, and of course he loved her and was faithful to her.

In Palestine, however, Israel was introduced to many other gods and started to worship them, offering them sacrifices of food and ornaments. The prophets described this worship of other gods as spiritual adultery.

The books of Moses and the historical books describe these same matters in different language; they portray God's relationship with Israel as a treaty covenant. Much of the book of Deuteronomy follows the normal structure of a treaty covenant, with a historical prologue (Deut 1-4), followed by stipulations of the covenant (Deut 5-26), then the names of divine witnesses (Deut 4:26; 26:16-19), and ending with blessings and curses (Deut 27-28). This covenant treaty is just like an ancient Near Eastern treaty in which both sides agree on what they will do (the stipulations) and the more powerful side makes promises for when these stipulations are kept and threats for when they are broken (the blessings and curses). They called this a "contract," which is often translated as "covenant"; the two words have the same meaning, and there is only one Hebrew word *(berith)* behind them both.

Some people think that a marriage should not be called a contract because it is a covenant. The difference is, they say, that a contract can be broken but a covenant can never end even if the stipulations are constantly being violated. They say that national treaties and trade agreements are "contracts," but when God makes an agreement with his people it should be called a "covenant." Such a covenant is seen preeminently in the "New Covenant" that is made with Judah and Israel (Jer 31:31), for which the New Testament is named.

There are very big problems with this idea, the biggest of which is that "covenant" and "contract" are both translations of the same Hebrew word, so the idea of a distinction does not exist in the Bible. Although it is true that the New Covenant is unbreakable and does not rely on our keeping the stipulations, this does not mean that every agreement that God makes is like this or that marriage is like this. God's first covenant or contract with Israel, which he made at Mt. Sinai, certainly had stipulations (the law) and curses and blessings that would result from violating or keeping these stipulations. Marriage is also regarded by Malachi as a contract that can be broken, and the prophets regarded God's marriage contract with Israel as breakable.

A BROKEN CONTRACT

An ancient treaty contract and an ancient marriage contract are both similar to a modern commercial contract. Both sides agree to stipulations (e.g., "you build this and I'll pay you") and make promises ("I'll pay you on time if you finish on time"), with threats of penalties ("there's a penalty of $1,000 if you don't finish on time").

Mrs. Hopeful asked Mr. Oddjob, the builder, to build her a sunroom by the end of June. Her daughter was getting married in eight weeks' time, on July 1, and the reception would be held in the sunroom and large garden at home. Mr. Oddjob was enthusiastic: "No problem, madam. My price, just for you, is $5,000."

"That's a deal," she said, "so long as it's finished by July 1."

"Don't worry," he assured her, "it'll only take twenty days." But he neglected to say that he would spread the twenty days over three months. When the wedding day arrived, there was nothing but a muddy building site that the guests had to tramp across to reach the garden.

The next day, Mrs. Hopeful called Mr. Oddjob: "You've broken our contract. I'll pay you $2,000 for your work so far, and I'll get someone else to finish the job."

"You can't do that!" he complained. "You agreed to a contract for the whole job." And that was just the start of a long story...

Who was in the right, Mrs. Hopeful or Mr. Oddjob? I think most fair-minded people would agree that Mrs. Hopeful had the right to end the contract because the builder broke one of the stipulations: that he would finish by July 1 (though a good lawyer might argue that she did not use the magical legal phrase "Time is of the essence"). In our law, as in ancient law, the victim of a broken contract can decide to end it, or the parties can decide to carry on in the hope that things will get better.

God's contract (or covenant) with Israel also had stipulations, promises and penalties. The stipulations were the Ten Commandments and the other laws; the promises were a peaceful life in the Promised Land he had given them; and the penalties were the removal of his protection and exile from that land. Sadly, as we know, the Israelites broke the commandments, so God sent them into exile, just as he said he would in the contract.

That is the way the historical books of the Old Testament treat the exile of Israel—as a broken treaty contract. But the prophets regarded God's relationship with Israel as a marriage contract. This contract was very similar: it too had stipulations, promises and penalties. The stipulations were the vows to feed, clothe and share conjugal love in faithfulness; the promise was a happy life together; and the penalty was divorce. Israel continually broke these stipulations until God eventually divorced her, and the prophets warned Judah that she was heading in the same direction. As Jeremiah said: "Judah saw that for all the adulteries of that faithless one, Israel, I had sent her away with a decree of divorce. Yet her treacherous sister Judah did not fear, but she too went and played the whore" (Jer 3:8).

ISRAEL'S BROKEN MARRIAGE VOWS

Ezekiel was particularly interested in the grounds for God's divorce. He warned Judah that she was going the same way as her sister kingdom of Israel (Ezek 23:30-33). God kept all four of his marriage vows: he loved Judah and gave her food and clothing fit for a queen (Ezek 16:8-13), and of course he was faithful to her. But, in contrast, Judah broke all four marriage vows: she did not return God's love; she committed adultery with idols (Ezek 16:15); she presented idols with the food that God had given her (Ezek 16:19); and she decorated idols with the clothing and jewels with which God had honored her (Ezek 16:16-18).

God warned Judah that he had already divorced Israel for these types of sins (Ezek 23:9). The remarkable message of the prophets was that although God had every right to divorce Judah, just as he had divorced her "sister" Israel, he decided to do something completely different. He decided to create a new covenant that would transform people from the inside. Unlike all God's previous covenants, and unlike any human covenant, this one could not be broken when one side failed to keep the stipulations, but it would continue unconditionally forever (Ezek 16:60-62). These prophecies were fulfilled in the New Testament (which is named for this new covenant) when Christ died for all sin. Even Israel was going to share in this restoration, not by remarrying God but by rejoining Judah to become a single new nation (Ezek 37:15-28).

Israel did not know anything about God's wonderful future plans while she was heading for divorce, and she stubbornly continued to break her marriage vows. All the prophets portray God acting in a forgiving and patient manner—he didn't divorce her immediately and gave her many chances to repent. But Israel, his wife, continued to sin, refusing to honor her vows, and God reluctantly had to divorce her. The marriage was broken and dead, and God merely carried out the legal formalities of divorce that recognized that fact.

GOD HATES DIVORCE

We know now why God says in Malachi that he "hates divorce"[3]: he knows from personal experience how much pain results from it. As he says in Malachi, divorce results from breaking marriage contract promises—promises to which God himself was a witness: "The Lord was witness between you and the wife of your youth, to whom you have been faithless, though she is your companion and your wife by covenant" (Mal 2:14).

God does not criticize the legal process of divorce or the person who carries it out; otherwise he would criticize himself, because he had to divorce Israel. God hates the breaking of marriage vows that *results* in divorce. He says that breaking these vows is being "faithless," because it breaks the marriage covenant or contract.

A marriage is ended by the person who breaks the marriage vows, not by the wronged person who decides to end the broken contract by enacting a divorce. Divorce is usually terrible for both partners, but remaining married can often be worse. Suffering continued neglect or abuse can be physically and emotionally damaging, and continuing unfaithfulness can bring the whole institution of marriage into disrepute.

CONCLUSION: PRACTICAL LAWS FOR A SINFUL WORLD

We have seen that, in the Old Testament, marriage is a contract, so it can be ended if one party breaks the stipulations that were agreed to in it, but the only person who has the right to end a contract is the victim of broken promises. They can decide to continue, or they can decide that enough is enough. The Old Testament thus gives us some very practical laws on divorce. People cannot divorce their husband or wife simply because they want to, but only if their spouse has broken their marriage vows. Divorce is not compulsory; the wronged partner also has the choice to forgive and carry on in the marriage.

Imagine the situation if Mrs. Hopeful had married Mr. Oddjob instead of employing him. They promise to feed, clothe, share conjugal love with and be faithful to each other. And imagine that he started hitting her or spending all the housekeeping money. Would she have the right to end the marriage contract? Under Old Testament law, yes. Or imagine that she started taking lovers and spending his money on them. Would he have the right to divorce her? Under Old Testament law, yes.

In the sad reality of this world, a marriage contract or covenant can most certainly be broken by partners who break their marriage vows. The Old Testament is aware of human sin and has practical laws to deal with its consequences. We will see that there is nothing to suggest that the New Testament is any less practical. We will see in chapter five that Jesus recognizes the necessity of divorce but says that we should avoid it whenever possible.

FURTHER READING

On the Three Grounds in Exodus 21:10-11

Instone-Brewer, David. *Divorce and Remarriage in the Bible.* Grand Rapids: Eerdmans, 2002. The second half of chapter 1, "The Ancient Near East," deals with this text in the ancient Near Eastern context. The middle section of chapter 5, "Rabbinic Teaching," deals with the way the Jews applied this text in their divorce laws.

Luck. William F. *Divorce and Remarriage: Recovering the Biblical View.* New York: Harper & Row, 1987. This text is often recognized by Jewish scholars as the basis for early Jewish divorce laws, but Luck is the only Christian I have found who discusses it with regard to New Testament teaching on divorce; see pp.31-34.

On God's Divorce in the Prophets

Cornes, Andrew. *Divorce and Remarriage: Biblical Principles and Pastoral Practice.* Grand Rapids: Eerdmans, 1993. Cornes deals with this material very well, though his conclusions are completely opposite to my own.

Instone-Brewer, David. *Divorce and Remarriage in the Bible.* Grand Rapids: Eerdmans, 2002. Chapter 3, "The Later Prophets," looks at the prophetic writings in some detail.

_____. "Three Weddings and a Divorce: God's Covenant with Israel, Judah and the Church." *Tyndale Bulletin* 47 (1996):1-26. Looks at the wider picture, including the New Testament church.

Ortlund, Raymond C. *God's Unfaithful Wife: A Biblical Theology of Spiritual Adultery.* Downers Grove, Ill.: InterVarsity Press, 1996. Covers the whole subject in great detail.

On Ancient Near Eastern Treaty Covenants

Walton, James H. *Ancient Israelite Literature in Its Cultural Context: A Survey of Parallels Between Biblical and Ancient Near Eastern Texts.* Grand Rapids: Zondervan, 1989. Chapter 4 is a good summary of the texts and how they compare to the Old Testament covenants.

4

THE CHURCH CAN'T DO WITHOUT IT

Jesus criticized those who abandoned Old Testament law.

The preceding chapters have shown us that the Old Testament has some very useful and practical things to say about divorce. But we live in the New Testament age, and many people would say that we have to put the Old Testament behind us. It's true that we cannot simply apply the Old Testament law as though nothing has changed, but Jesus called us to take note of every letter of God's law, so we cannot simply ignore it.

You may have heard the following story. I had already heard it in Christian circles when a Jewish professor from Jerusalem told it to me as something that actually happened to a friend of his in New York. Perhaps I have found the origin of the story, or perhaps his friend was just passing it on as a good story.

A semireligious Jewish family went to a new synagogue, and the eldest son, Adam, reluctantly attended the sabbath school. Afterward, over lunch, his father asked Adam what he had learned. At first he was reticent to say anything, but after thinking for a bit he replied enthusiastically: "We learned about how Moses took his people across the Red Sea and defeated the Egyptians. He lined up his tanks against them, then sent amphibious craft onto the Red Sea to start building a pontoon. When it was finished, the Israelites all ran across while their fighter planes gave them cover. The Egyptians chased them, but Moses blew up the pontoon and the Egyptians all drowned."

"Now, Adam," said his father, "I'm sure that's not what the teacher told you!"

"Well, no, not quite," admitted Adam, "but if I told you what he really said, you'd never believe it!"

APPLYING THE OLD TESTAMENT TODAY

The Old Testament is just too old for some people. The culture it was addressing is now ancient, and the laws it contains are largely unworkable today. No one today can imagine putting a suspected adulterous woman through a life-threatening ordeal to see if she is guilty or not (as in Num 5) or treating a woman as unclean for forty days after she has given birth to a boy, or eighty days if it is a girl (as in Lev 12). We do not sell our children as slaves (as at the start of Ex 21) or buy foreign slaves and leave them to our children in our wills (as in Lev 25:44-46).

Our culture is very different now—thanks largely to the effects of the gospel—and many of these Old Testament laws no longer apply. Even some New Testament ethics are now out of date: no Christian leader would send a slave back to his owner as Paul did with Onesimus, even if the leader was able to give him a letter for his master that was as wise and culturally trans- forming as the letter Paul sent to Philemon. And although some churches still insist that women keep their heads covered in church, the reason for this is no longer a question of common decency as it was in the days of the New Testament, when uncovering one's hair was equivalent to wearing a bikini or less.

Despite the cultural changes, however, believers today would not think of putting aside the whole New Testament. Yet some Christians do act as though the whole Old Testament can be ignored.

THE MORAL AND CEREMONIAL LAWS

There are three main ways by which we can decide what parts of the Old Testament laws still apply to Christians today. The most common method is to say that the New Testament has left behind the ceremonial laws (such as sacrifices, food laws and cleanliness issues), while it has inherited the moral laws (such as the Ten Commandments and the other moral demands of Moses and the prophets). The rationale for this difference is the death of Christ, because the ceremonial law was completely fulfilled by his sacrifice.

This tidy division between moral and ceremonial law is a good rule of thumb, but it is sometimes difficult to know into which category a particular law fits. For example, many believers would regard tithing as a moral principle, although very few apply the Old Testament stipulations about tithing one tenth for religious workers (the Levites, as in Num 18:20-24) and a *second* tenth for celebrating religious festivals and for the poor (as prescribed in Deut 14:22-29). Similarly, the details of punishments for disobeying moral principles should be ignored, such as the taking of "eye for eye" or executing a rebellious son who is a glutton and drunkard (see Deut 21:18-21).

Another method is to say that Christians should follow the moral *principles* in the Old Testament but not the *details*—the quantities, dates and punishments that belong to a former age. As we will see, Jesus applied the principles rather than the details of Old Testament law, so this method could be said to be following his example.

A third method is to say that Christians should ignore any Old Testament laws that are not specifically mentioned in the New Testament. Such an argument from silence, as we will see in chapter seven, should be used only when a silence is surprising. For example, it is not surprising that the New Testament should fail to repeat every moral command contained in the Old Testament, because the Old Testament is much longer than the New Testament and because it has a lot more passages relating to moral behavior. Therefore most Christians conclude that we have inherited all the Old Testament moral principles that are not specifically denied in the New Testament.

The two Testaments are also different in style: the commands contained in the Old Testament are mainly laws and religious rules, whereas the New Testament's commands concern mainly morals and guidelines for living. This is because the Old Testament was largely written by law-makers and prophets for the guidance of a nation, whereas the New Testament was written for churches and individual believers who needed guidance about how to live within the laws of whatever nation they found themselves in. This difference has made some people see the religion of the Old Testament as legalistic and mainly concerned with punishment and see the New Testament as full of grace and forgiveness. This is nonsense, of course, because God has not changed: he was no less forgiving in the Old Testament than he is now, though the basis of his forgiveness—the death of Jesus—is a New Testament event.

It is ironic that the New Testament, which emphasizes God's grace and forgiveness, is usually regarded as much harsher with regard to victims of marital abuse. The traditional interpretation assumes that Jesus introduced a new and stricter policy on divorce that overturned the Old Testament principle that a victim has the right to bring their suffering to an end. But if we examine Jesus' attitude toward the Old

Testament, we find that he had a very high regard for it, so we would not expect him to overturn one of its important moral principles.

JESUS' VIEW OF THE OLD TESTAMENT

Jesus regarded the Old Testament as God's Word and said that every letter was important:

> Do not think that I have come to abolish the Law or the Prophets; I have not come to abolish them but to fulfill them. For truly, I say to you, until heaven and earth pass away, not an iota, not a dot, will pass from the Law until all is accomplished. Therefore whoever relaxes one of the least of these commandments and teaches others to do the same will be called least in the kingdom of heaven, but whoever does them and teaches them will be called great in the kingdom of heaven. (Mt 5:17-19)

Jesus fulfilled the ceremonial parts of the law on the cross, but he wants us to fulfill the moral parts of the law, and he even said that he wanted us to be perfect like our Father (Mt 5:48). He never told anyone to break an Old Testament law. Even though the Pharisees accused him and his disciples of breaking the law, they only broke traditions that the Pharisees had *added* to the Old Testament.

In Matthew 5, where some people think that Jesus overturns Old Testament laws in his teaching, he actually does the reverse: he affirms the principles of these laws and widens their application. He makes a distinction between the original law and the new interpretations by which that law has been changed, and while rejecting the new interpretations, he affirms the original old law:

- He affirms the law against murder and applies its principle by saying that if murder that arises from hatred is wrong, then murderous hatred is also wrong (Mt 5:21-26).

- He affirms the law against adultery by saying that if adultery comes from illicit lust, then illicit lust is wrong. And if illicit lust comes from lustful looking, then lustful looking is also wrong (Mt 5:27-30).

- He affirms the law of divorce in Deuteronomy 24:1 (Mt 5:31-32); we will look at this more closely, especially in chapter five.

- He affirms the law against making false oaths to God, saying that if it is wrong to lie to God, then it is wrong to speak any lies (Mt 5:33-37).

- He affirms the Old Testament limitations to the laws of compensation (for example, if someone knocks your tooth out, your revenge may not be greater than knocking his tooth out) by saying that if the law tells us to restrict our wish for revenge, then we should avoid revenge altogether (Mt 5:38-42).

- He affirms the law to love your neighbor and rejects the words "and hate your enemy," which some people had added to this command (Mt 5:43-47).

JESUS HIGHLIGHTS PRINCIPLES, NOT DETAILS

As well as endorsing these laws, Jesus amplifies them by identifying the principles behind them and applying those principles to the whole of life. The principle behind "You shall not murder" and "You shall not commit adultery" is to avoid the causes of these sins as well as the sins themselves. The principle behind the importance of honesty in oaths and loving one's neighbor is that these attitudes should encompass the whole of life, so that all our statements are honest and all our relationships, even with our enemies, are governed by love.

Jesus never criticizes what the Old Testament says, though he frequently criticizes the way people interpret it. He condemns the way some people tried to sidestep the command about oaths by claiming that they were not making a real oath if they swore "by heaven" or "by Jerusalem" (Mt 5:34-35), and he criticizes the way people had diluted the command to "love your neighbor" by saying that this did not include enemies. And as we will see in chapter five, Jesus reproves those who wrongly interpreted an Old Testament ruling about divorce so that they could invent a new ground for divorce.

It is clear, then, that Jesus did not reject the Old Testament, but he did reject new interpretations that had diluted the Old Testament's moral principles. He emphasizes the importance of the Old Testament law by saying, "Whoever relaxes one of the least of these commandments and teaches others to do the same will be called least in the kingdom of heaven" (Mt 5:19). Jesus does not mean that we should keep all the *details* of Old Testament law in exactly the way it was prescribed for the nation of Israel in the ancient Near Eastern world. We can see from the way he discusses these various commandments in Matthew 5 that he was concerned with the principles behind the laws rather than the details. Therefore we can also legitimately ignore the details of Old Testament law, but we may not neglect any of the principles.

There are a few Old Testament principles we can ignore, such as laws about how to treat our slaves, because (thank God) most countries are now free of this scourge. But this does not give us a reason to ignore the principles about divorce, because the world of marriage and sexual relations has not changed very much. Jesus taught that Old Testament moral principles should be applied much *more* strictly by Christians—not *less.*

THE BASIS OF MODERN LAWS

Many of the laws forming the basis of our modern legal systems and Christian ethics occur only in the Old Testament. Without the Old Testament, in fact, the Bible would have no word of criticism for either rape or consensual sex outside of marriage. These are dealt with in Deuteronomy 22:23-29 with clarity and fairness, though the degrees of punishment would not be appropriate in modern societies. Many other branches of modern law are not only illustrated in the Old Testament but established on principles that were inspired by Old Testament law. Our ancestors had a very high regard for God's law, and they did not reject its principles simply because they were not found in the New Testament.

One chapter in particular, Exodus 21, has provided the foundations for our modern laws on murder and injury. It established the differences between accidental killing, un-premeditated murder and pre meditated mur-der (Ex 21:12-14)—categories that are at the heart of murder laws in most modern societies. Our laws of injury and compensation are based on the principle that recompense should reflect the amount of damage done (Ex 21:23-25) and on the categories of deliberate harm, accidental harm and consequential harm that are defined in this chapter (Ex 21:18-22). This same chapter also establishes principles about accidental harm by animals under someone's care and makes a distinction between foresee-able injury and unforeseeable accidents, with higher fines for those who have not taken the necessary precautions (Ex 21:29). Although modern law has multiplied the details into bewildering complexities, the foundations are still recognizable in Exodus 21.

Exodus 21 is also where we find the moral principle that a victim of marital neglect or abuse can choose to end the marriage. Bearing in mind that other principles in the same passage form the foundation of our national laws, we should think very carefully before we choose to simply dismiss it. Likewise the church should not decide to teach the Old Testament morals about sex outside marriage and yet reject its morals about neglect or abuse within marriage.

CONCLUSION: KEEPING THE SPIRIT OF THE LAW

God has given us his laws to help us in a practical way. Imagine what would happen if God's marriage laws were kept without exception for just one generation: all sexually transmitted diseases would be wiped out forever! So as well as providing a model for the world of the ancient Near East, the Old Testament law provides a model for our modern world—because human nature has not changed very much.

In the following chapters we will look at what the New Testament says about the specific Old Testament law concerning the victim of marital neglect or abuse. As I have mentioned, some interpreters say that Jesus' teaching brought the Old Testament law about divorce to an end, but we will see in the following chapters that Jesus and Paul actually *affirmed* it and that Jesus criticized the Pharisees for changing it.

FURTHER READING

On the Old Testament in Relation to the New

Baker, David. *Two Testaments, One Bible: A Study of the Theological Relationship Between the Old and New Testaments.* Downers Grove, Ill.: InterVarsity Press, 1991. Emphasizes the intrinsic links between the Testaments.

Rushdoony, R.J. *The Institutes of Biblical Law.* Phillipsburg, N.J.: Presbyterian & Reformed, 1973. Rushdoony tries to apply virtually all the Old Testament to Christian lifestyle. This is an extreme example of using the Old Testament, but it is interesting to see how much he can achieve.

Wenham, John. *Christ and the Bible.* Grand Rapids: Baker, 1994. Shows how Jesus regarded the Old Testament as real history.

5

DIVORCE ON DEMAND?

Jesus taught us to forgive the repentant partner.

A man in Dubai divorced his wife in 2001 by a totally new method—he sent her a text message on her phone. She had failed to turn up on time to make his tea, so he texted her: "You're late. I divorce you." This was the third time he'd told her he would divorce her, and according to Islamic law if a man tells his wife "I divorce you" three times, this is all that is needed: the wife is legally divorced when she receives that third message.

The woman in Dubai could not believe that she could be divorced by a text message, so she took it to a Muslim court, but the court upheld the man's right. Any Muslim man is allowed to divorce his wife in this way without needing to show that she has done anything wrong. A Muslim woman, however, is not allowed to divorce her husband at all.

A NEW TYPE OF DIVORCE, FOR MEN ONLY

Jewish men are also able to get a divorce quite easily, without needing to cite any grounds. Instead of saying "I divorce you" three times, a Jewish man has to write out a divorce certificate and give it to his wife; as soon as she receives it, she is legally divorced. As in Islamic law, only men can initiate divorce, and it is a groundless divorce—the man does not have to show that his wife has done anything wrong. The groundless divorce also means that the woman cannot defend herself.

Although the divorce certificate is part of the law of Moses in Deuteronomy 24:1, this groundless divorce "for men only" did not become available until about the time of Jesus' birth. Before this, both Jewish men and women could divorce partners who broke their marriage obligations, as defined in the Old Testament. We also saw in chapter three that the Old Testament allowed only the wronged partner to initiate a divorce. If a woman did not feed, clothe or share conjugal love with her husband faithfully, he could divorce her, and likewise, if a man did not give his wife money for food or clothing and did not share conjugal love with her, then she could divorce him. These grounds for divorce (based on Ex 21:10-11) were in use until about A.D.70, but by the time that Jesus was preaching, in about A.D.30, they were being used only rarely. During Jesus' lifetime the new groundless divorce gradually grew in popularity, until, by about the end of the first century, it had totally replaced divorces based on Old Testament grounds.

This new type of divorce was invented by a rabbi called Hillel, who lived a few decades before Jesus, and was called the "Any Cause" divorce. The phrase that inspired it is in Deuteronomy 24:1, where a man divorces his wife for "a cause of sexual immorality": "When a man takes a wife and marries her, if then she finds no favor in his eyes because he has found a cause of sexual immorality in her, ... he writes her a certificate of divorce."[1] Hillel asked, why did Moses use the phrase "cause of sexual immorality" when he could simply have said "sexual immorality"? Hillel reasoned that the seemingly superfluous word *cause* must refer to another, different ground for divorce, and since this other ground is simply called a "cause," he concluded that it meant *any* cause.[2]

THE "ANY CAUSE" DIVORCE

Hillel therefore thought that two types of divorce were taught in Deuteronomy 24:1: one for "sexual immorality" (adultery) and one they named "Any Cause." The Hillelite rabbis came to two main conclusions about the new "Any Cause" form of divorce. First, they concluded that an "Any Cause" divorce could be carried out only by men, because the example case in Deuteronomy 24:1 involves a man who divorces his wife. Second, they said that it could be used for any cause—such as the wife's burning a meal—so although the "Any Cause" divorce was theoretically based on some kind of fault, this fault could be such a small thing that it was, in effect, a groundless divorce.

The "Any Cause" type of divorce soon became very popular—especially because you didn't need any proof and didn't have to present your case in court. There was no need to try to prove in court that your wife had neglected you—a very embarrassing process, because all your neighbors would find out the details you had been hiding from them for years! All you needed to do to carry out an "Any Cause" divorce was write out a divorce certificate and give it to your wife.

The only times when the "Any Cause" divorce was not more beneficial for the man were those few occasions when he could *prove* that his wife had been unfaithful—and especially when this unfaithfulness became public knowledge. He could get his revenge on his wife by taking her to court to obtain a divorce on the Old Testament ground of unfaithfulness. There was also a financial advantage for the man in this situation, because if he could prove that his wife had been unfaithful, he did not have to give her the marriage inheritance *(ketubah)* that he had promised to her when they married.

Despite the disadvantages to them, many women were also in favor of the "Any Cause" divorce, because it meant they would probably be able to claim their marriage inheritance (which, in many cases, was large enough to live on). If a wife was taken to court on the Old Testament grounds of being neglectful or abusive, she ran the risk of financial penury, because the court could decide to remove some or all of her marriage inheritance from her. A court hearing also, of course, meant public shame and humiliation.

Very soon the "Any Cause" divorce had almost completely replaced the traditional Old Testament types of divorce. We can see how respectable it had become by the time of Jesus' birth because Joseph considered using this means to break off his betrothal to Mary: "Her husband Joseph, being a just man and unwilling to put her to shame, resolved to divorce her quietly" (Mt 1:19). Joseph did not want to put Mary through the disgrace of a public trial, so he decided to use the quiet "Any Cause" divorce that did not require any proof of wrongdoing. Matthew considered that this would be the action of a "just man," because Joseph could have ensured that he didn't have to pay Mary's marriage inheritance if he had decided to prove her guilty of adultery in court.

NOTHING EXCEPT "SEXUAL IMMORALITY"

Not everyone accepted this new type of divorce. The disciples of Shammai, a rival of Hillel who often disagreed with him, said that Hillel had interpreted the Scriptures wrongly and that the whole phrase "a cause of sexual immorality" meant nothing more than the ground of sexual immorality; it did not mean two grounds, sexual immorality and "Any Cause." They summarized their opinion by saying that, on the basis of Deuteronomy 24:1, "a man should not divorce his wife except he has found 'sexual immorality' in her."[3]

The interpretation of this short phrase, "a cause of sexual immorality," was a matter of huge public debate. The disciples of Shammai wanted people to restrict themselves to divorces based on the Old Testament grounds—unfaithfulness in Deuteronomy 24:1 and neglect of food, clothing or conjugal love in Exodus 21:10-11. But the common people preferred Hillel's interpretation, which added the "Any Cause" divorce.

The ordinary people were not too interested in the intricate arguments over these interpretations, but because divorce was common in first-century Judaism, they did have to know the basics of the debate so that they could pick the right lawyers. Most people would have had a friend or relative who had been through a divorce, and they would therefore have known that Hillel allowed "Any Cause" divorces and that Shammai said that "a cause of sexual immorality" meant nothing except divorce for sexual immorality. In the same way, nowadays, when divorce is also very common, most people recognize legal jargon like "spousal support" and "custody" without necessarily understanding their detailed meanings.

ASKING JESUS' OPINION

Therefore, by the time of Jesus, almost every divorce was an "Any Cause" divorce, but the rabbis were still arguing about it. These rabbis decided to ask Jesus what he thought: "Is it lawful to divorce one's wife for 'any cause'?" (see Section "REREADING THE GOSPEL PASSAGE" in Chapter 5). This verse is normally translated "Is it lawful to divorce one's wife for any cause?" or "...for any reason?" As I mentioned in chapter one, when I was rereading these familiar words with the benefit of my rabbinic studies, I found that I was understanding the text differently. I remembered that the Hillelites called their new form of divorce the "Any Cause" divorce—a legal term that was used by other Jews such as Philo and Josephus as well as by the rabbis themselves.[4] The identification of this term was not my own, new discovery—many people had already written a great deal about the Hillelite divorce. Yet this fact had never been taken into account by any of the biblical translations.

According to the standard translations, such as "Is it lawful to divorce one's wife for any cause?" the Pharisees appear to be asking

Jesus if he thought divorce itself was lawful or not. But the question "Is it lawful to divorce?" would have been an illogical one. To the Jews *divorce* referred to a procedure that is defined in the law of Moses—and the law of Moses cannot be "unlawful"! However, if you translate the question "Is it lawful to divorce one's wife for 'Any Cause'?" it makes perfect sense. The rabbis wanted to know what Jesus thought about the new "Any Cause" type of divorce and how he interpreted Deuteronomy 24:1.

Actually in the account of this episode in Mark, the rabbis do appear to ask the illogical version of the question, "Is it lawful for a man to divorce his wife?" (Mk 10:2). There is a simple explanation for this: anyone reading Mark in the first century would have mentally added "for 'Any Cause'" to complete the question, because everyone at the time was talking about it. It was like someone today who asks, "Is it lawful for a sixteen-year-old to drink?" In itself this is an illogical question, because without anything to drink we dehydrate and die. Therefore we mentally add "alcoholic beverages" to the end of the question to make sense of it, but it would be pedantic to actually ask the question in this form. In exactly the same way a first-century

Jew would have mentally added "for 'Any Cause'" to the end of the otherwise illogical question in Mark 10.

UNDERSTANDING THE JARGON

The account of this debate with the Pharisees is highly abbreviated because it had to fit it into a short Gospel. Throughout the Gospels, speeches are shortened to a couple of sentences, and fascinating incidents that might otherwise have taken a whole book to recount are summarized in just one paragraph.

These shortened accounts did not matter for a first-century Jew, who knew the context and the Old Testament very well, but they sometimes make things a little obscure for a modern reader. Therefore we have to work hard at unpacking the abbreviated account of what Jesus and the Pharisees said. Although superfluous phrases like "for 'Any Cause'" were usually omitted, Matthew decided to state the question in full in order to help his readers; he was writing his Gospel a little later than Mark, at a time when this rabbinic debate had become less well known.

Jesus was asked if he agreed with the new Hillelite "Any Cause" divorce, but he wasn't really interested in this debate and was more concerned, as we will see below, to tell the Hillelites and Shammaites where they had both gone wrong. When the rabbis eventually got Jesus back to their question, he gave the same straightforward interpretation of Deuteronomy 24:1 that Shammai taught; that is, he said that the phrase "a cause of sexual immorality" meant "nothing except 'sexual immorality.'" And to emphasize this, Jesus said that if someone got divorced on the basis of any other interpretation (i.e., the "Any Cause" divorce), they were not properly divorced, and so if they remarried they would be committing adultery (Mt 19:9).

Most interpreters have not recognized that Jesus is quoting the rabbinic legal phrases "divorce for 'Any Cause'" and "nothing except 'sexual immorality.'" As a result, they think that Jesus was asked "Is it ever lawful to divorce?" and that he answered "No—except in cases of sexual immorality."

Not knowing the meaning of the rabbinic legal phrase "nothing except 'sexual immorality,'" these interpreters have tried to find out what "sexual immorality" meant by looking carefully at the Greek word *porneia*. Some interpreted it as "adultery" and others as "sex before marriage" (especially during betrothal) or as "incest." These definitions are actually all correct, because *porneia* is a very general word that means all these things as well as any other type of sexual immorality, including visiting prostitutes (as in 1 Cor 6:13-18). Jesus (or his translator) used it because it was the best translation of the Hebrew word for general "sexual immorality" *('ervah)* in the rabbinic legal phrase "except 'sexual immorality.'"

Jesus was using the same language as the people he was speaking to, and he was refer-ring to biblical texts and legal discussions they all knew about. He was not speaking a new language that only he knew, so we should ask ourselves not what Jesus meant by *porneia* but what his *hearers* or the original *readers* would have understood by *porneia* or by the phrase "except for 'sexual immorality.'" This raises the whole question of how God communicates through Scripture to a multitude of generations, which we will look at in chapter twelve.

ANSWERING THEIR QUESTION

Jesus was answering their question in plain language, and he wasn't making a universal statement. Therefore when he said "nothing except 'sexual immorality,'" he was saying that the phrase "a cause of sexual immorality" did not include the extra ground of "Any Cause," and he didn't mean "there is no divorce ever, in any part of the Bible, except on the ground of 'sexual immorality.'" If he had been making this universal statement, he would have been contradicting Paul, who allowed divorce for abandonment (1 Cor 7:15—as we will see in chapter six).

Imagine that my wife is dressing to go out and is wondering whether to wear a jacket over her dress. She asks me, "Should I wear the jacket?" I answer, "I think you should just wear the dress."

Then imagine my surprise when she comes downstairs wearing the dress and nothing else—no shoes, no stockings or anything—explaining, "Well, you said I should 'just wear the dress.'" This is exactly what some people do to Jesus' reply, "Nothing except 'sexual immorality.'" Instead of regarding this as an answer to a specific question about the grounds for divorce in Deuteronomy 24:1, they regard it as a universal statement about the whole of Scripture.

Jesus gave the Pharisees a straightforward answer about where he stood in their debate, but actually he was not very interested in this subject. He was much more interested in marriage than in divorce, so although he gave this answer in Matthew 19:9, he didn't do so until he had spent the intervening verses talking about marriage, and specifically about matters where he disagreed with both Hillelites and Shammaites.

JESUS' OTHER TEACHING ON MARRIAGE AND DIVORCE

Jesus was determined to tell his listeners where they had all gone wrong with regard to marriage and divorce—so he went back to basics!

Polygamy was allowed by most Jews in the first century (except for the sect at Qumran and a few progressive Jews who taught against it) and was widely practiced in Palestine—the only place where Roman law allowed it. Jesus tells his questioners, however, that monogamy was the biblical ideal from the beginning. Jesus alludes to Genesis 2:24 when he says, "So they are no longer two but one flesh." He deliberately includes the word *two,* which is not actually found in the Hebrew text, although it was often added there when the Old Testament was translated into other languages such as Greek and Aramaic. The fact that Jesus includes the word two is therefore very significant. He also points out that God made the first human beings "male and female"—both singular—and thus reminds his questioners that the perfect marriage in Eden involved only two people.

Jesus continues by stressing that God intended marriage to be life-long and that marriage breakup is a tragedy. Therefore instead of divorcing an erring partner, he says, you should try to forgive them. Jesus demonstrates how serious it is to break up a marriage by giving a commandment: "What therefore God has joined together, let not man separate" (Mt 19:6).

The Pharisees think that they have a clever answer for this: they say that sometimes Moses instructed that you *must* divorce a wife. They believed that divorce was compulsory if a woman committed adultery, because Deuteronomy 24:1 says that a man should give a divorce certificate to a wife guilty of "sexual immorality." So they argue with Jesus: "Why then did Moses *command* one to give a certificate of divorce?" (Mt 19:7). Jesus replies, "Moses *allowed* you to divorce your wives" (Mt 19:8)—that is, he did not command it but allowed it. It was not *compulsory,* although it was permissible.

DIVORCE ONLY FOR "HARDHEARTEDNESS"

Jesus also says that God does not want us to divorce if we can avoid it, even in the case of adultery; he wants us to forgive an erring partner rather than divorce them. "But surely there's a limit to the number of times we have to forgive?" we say—and I'm sure that the Pharisees also said this, or at least they thought it. So Jesus explains further: "Moses allowed divorce for *hardheartedness.*"

The Pharisees knew immediately what he meant, but we are not so familiar with the Old Testament, so we have to work at it a bit. *Hardheartedness* means "stubbornness," and the corresponding Greek word had been invented by the translators of the Septuagint, the official Jewish translation of the Old Testament into Greek. It occurs frequently in the Septuagint but does not occur in ordinary Greek except when people were quoting the Old Testament. So Jesus is presumably alluding to an Old Testament text—but which one? This was not a difficult question for the Pharisees, many of whom knew the Old Testament by heart, because *hardheartedness* occurs in only one place in the context of divorce—where Jeremiah warns Judah that God might divorce them as he divorced Israel: "Circumcise yourselves to your Lord, and circumcise your hardheartedness" (Jer 4:4 LXX).

Jeremiah has described Israel as God's wife at the beginning of this section (Jer 2:1) and has said that she committed adultery with other gods (Jer 2:20-26) so that God was forced to divorce her (Jer 3:1-8), as we saw in some detail in chapter three. Jeremiah warns Judah that she is going the same way as her sister nation, Israel (Jer 3:10-14), and that she is being hardhearted—stubborn—in her adultery (Jer 4:3-4).

Jesus says that marriage was not like this "from the beginning" (Mt 19:8). In Eden there was no sin to break up marriages, and therefore there was no need for divorce. But when sin came and marriages started going wrong, Moses "allowed" divorce for broken marriage vows (Mt 19:8). Jesus thought that people were being too quick to divorce, so he reminds them that Moses meant divorce to occur only when there was "hardheartedness"—that is, a stubborn refusal to repent and stop breaking marriage vows.

Jesus says elsewhere that we should forgive people if they sin against us and repent: "If he sins against you seven times in the day, and turns to you seven times, saying, 'I repent,' you must forgive him" (Lk 17:4). In marriage, too, we should forgive a partner who sins and repents. However many times they break their vows, we should forgive them if they repent and want to change their ways. We should consider divorce only if they continually break their vows with hardheartedness—if they stubbornly continue without repenting or trying to change. God found himself in this position when Israel constantly and unrepentantly went running after other gods, until eventually God, who hates divorce, had to divorce her for hardhearted adultery.

DROPPING THE BOMBSHELL

The disciples were utterly shocked at this teaching about forgiveness and at Jesus' rejection of the "Any Cause" type of divorce. Suddenly they realized that marriage is much more serious than they had thought and that they could not get divorced whenever they wished. They said, "If such is the case of a man with his wife, it is better not to marry" (Mt 19:10).

At this point Jesus showed how profoundly different his teaching was from the rest of

Judaism—he told his disciples that marriage is optional. All Jews regarded marriage as compulsory because of the command in Scripture, "Be fruitful and multiply" (Gen 1:28). Even the men of the Qumran sect, who tried to avoid women, got married for about five years when they were twenty, in order to fulfill this command. So when Jesus said that some "have made themselves eunuchs for the sake of the kingdom of heaven" (Mt 19:12), he was disagreeing with every Jew alive, so far as we know.

But the most shocking part of Jesus' teaching, as far as the general public was concerned, was his rejection of the "Any Cause" divorces. It meant that men could divorce their wives only on specific biblical grounds; they could not simply decide they didn't like her looks or her cooking anymore. And furthermore, Jesus said that they should forgive a partner who repented, and although he did allow divorce, he said that it should be only a very last resort.

Jesus did not just say that "Any Cause" divorces were invalid, but he emphasized their invalidity by saying that people with "Any Cause" divorces were not really divorced at all. Therefore, if they remarried after this type of divorce, they were actually committing adultery because they were still married to their previous partner.

REREADING THE GOSPEL PASSAGE

Much of what I have unpacked here is difficult to follow in the Gospels, because the Gospel writers could not record everything verbatim and they removed anything that was obvious. Having unpacked it, we should have a clearer idea of how a first-century reader understood this passage when they read or heard it. I will now go through it again (quoting the English Standard Version, which is a very accurate scholarly translation), in order to put all these details together.

The passage starts as some rabbis, probably Hillelites, asked Jesus if he accepted the "Any Cause" divorces as in Deuteronomy 24:1: "And Pharisees came up to him and tested him by asking, 'Is it lawful to divorce one's wife for any cause?'" (Mt 19:3).

Jesus wanted to talk about other things that he thought were more important. First, a man should marry only one wife, as in Eden. "He answered, 'Have you not read that he who created them from the beginning made them male and female, and said, "Therefore a man shall leave his father and his mother and hold fast to his wife, and they shall become one flesh"? So they are no longer two but one flesh'" (Mt 19:4-6).

Jesus also said that breaking up a marriage was very serious, because God has heard the couple's wedding vows and joined them with a blessing, as he did in Eden: "What therefore God has joined together, let not man separate" (Mt 19:6).

The rabbis brought Jesus back to their question by saying that a divorce certificate is *commanded* by Scripture in cases of adultery (Deut 24:1): "They said to him, 'Why then did Moses command one to give a certificate of divorce and to send her away?'"

Jesus said that divorce was never compulsory, and we should not divorce anyone unless they are hardhearted—stubbornly unrepentant, like adulterous Judah in Jeremiah 4:4. People are no longer sinless, as they were in Eden. "He said to them, 'Because of your hardness of heart Moses allowed you to divorce your wives, but from the beginning it was not so'" (Mt 19:8).[5]

Coming back to the original question, Jesus said that there was no ground for divorce in Deuteronomy 24:1 except sexual immorality, so divorces for "Any Cause" (on which virtually all divorces were based at that time) were invalid: "And I say to you: whoever divorces his wife, except for sexual immorality, and marries another, commits adultery" (Mt 19:9).

The disciples were shocked that divorce is so difficult. "The disciples said to him, 'If such is the case of a man with his wife, it is better not to marry'" (Mt 19:10).

Jesus answered that marriage is not compulsory, and it is not for everyone. "But he said to them, 'Not everyone can receive this saying, but only those to whom it is given. For there are eunuchs who have been so from birth, and there are eunuchs who have been made eunuchs by men, and there are eunuchs who have made themselves eunuchs for the sake of the kingdom of heaven. Let the one who is able to receive this receive it'" (Mt 19:11-12).

Mark's version is more difficult to understand because it is more highly abbreviated than Matthew's. The main differences are two phrases "for 'Any Cause'" and "nothing except 'sexual immorality,'" which are found in both of Matthew's accounts (Mt 19:3-12; 5:31-32) but not in those of Mark or Luke (Mk 10:2-12; Lk 16:18). Did Mark (and perhaps Luke) remove these well-known phrases because they were not necessary for his readership? Or did Matthew add them in order to help his readers understand the debate? I think both happened. Mark wrote first and abbreviated the debate as much as possible, but Matthew wrote later, when the debate was more or less over and was less well known. He knew his readers might get confused, so he helped them out by putting a few details back in.

SUMMARIZING JESUS' TEACHING

A summary, for a modern generation, of Jesus' teaching during this debate would be something like this: All divorces based on "Any Cause" (i.e., groundless divorces) are invalid, because the phrase "a cause of sexual immorality" (Deut 24:1) means nothing more than "sexual immorality." Moses never *commanded* divorce but *allowed* us to divorce a partner who is hardhearted (who unrepentantly breaks marriage vows, as in Jer 3-4).

Matthew and Luke both summarized this debate on divorce in one sentence and had to decide which aspects of Jesus' teaching to emphasize: his teaching on monogamy, on marriage not being compulsory, on divorce not being compulsory for adultery, on his opposition to "Any Cause" divorces, or his plea that we avoid divorce unless the erring partner is sinning "hardheartedly"?

Both Matthew and Luke picked the element that was most shocking for ordinary Jews: Jesus' rejection of the "Any Cause" type of divorce. This affected any family with a divorcee in it—which probably included most families in the land. It affected only those divorces that were based on "Any Cause," but since this type of divorce had already almost totally replaced the other types of divorce, the Evangelists could say, for the sake of abbreviation, that Jesus was talking about "everyone who divorces." Jesus had expressed this part of his teaching in a shocking and memorable way, saying that remarriage after this type of divorce was technically adultery, and they retained this in their summary versions:

> Everyone who divorces his wife and marries another commits adultery, and he who

marries a woman divorced from her husband commits adultery. (Lk 16:18)

But I say to you that everyone who divorces his wife, except on the ground of
sexual immorality, makes her commit
adultery. And whoever marries a divorced
woman commits adultery. (Mt 5:32)

These two texts look at the issue from several
different viewpoints, but they come to the
same conclusion. They both say that any remarriage would be adulterous because their divorces are invalid and so they are still married
to their former partners. The point is that Jesus
was so intractably against the "Any Cause" divorces that he said they were completely invalid.

QUESTIONS JESUS DOES NOT ANSWER

What should divorcees do if they have already
remarried? Should they get divorced from their
new partner and remarry their former spouse?
Jesus does not tell his disciples, or if he did,
the Gospels do not record it. Fortunately for
us, Paul does cover this type of problem, as
we shall see in chapter ten.

We would also like to know what Jesus thought about other biblical grounds for divorce. We know that he rejected the new non-biblical "Any Cause" divorces and that he accepted divorce for adultery, as in Deuteronomy 24:1, but we do not know what he thought about the three grounds for divorce in Exodus 21:10-11 because no one asked him about this text—or if they did, the Gospel writers did not think his teaching on this was significant enough to include in their short accounts. I would guess that for these grounds, as for adultery, he would counsel forgiveness rather than divorce, unless the spouse was sinning hardheartedly, but again, we have to look to Paul in chapters six and eight to fill in this gap in our knowledge.

We might also ask, How did the church misunderstand Jesus' teaching for so long? How come no one remembered about "Any Cause" divorces? We will look at this in chapter twelve.

We found in this chapter that Jesus laid the foundations for a new approach to divorce. He did not replace the Old Testament or rewrite it, but he emphasized its principles and compassion, saying that the injured partner should forgive the partner who breaks their marriage vows and then repents, and that you should

divorce only a partner who sins in a hardhearted way—one who breaks their vows stubbornly
and unrepentantly.

FURTHER READING

On Jewish Customs and Rabbinic Debates

Amram, D.W. "Divorce." In *Jewish Encyclopedia.*
12 vols., 4:624-28. New York: Funk &
Wagnalls, 1905. Amram provides a more
traditional Jewish view of Jewish literature. The
later rabbis in the Talmud misunderstood
Shammai's position (see my chapter seven),
and this article reflects that misunderstanding.

Instone-Brewer, David. *Divorce and Remarriage
in the Bible.* Grand Rapids: Eerdmans, 2002.
Chapter 5, "Rabbinic Teaching," summarizes
the evidence from ancient Jewish sources.

Isaksson, Abel. *Marriage and Ministry in the
New Temple. A Study with Special Reference
to Mt. 19.13[sic]-12 and 1 Cor. 11.3-16.* Lund:
Gleerup, 1965. The Dead Sea sect's teaching
has been reevaluated recently, but this remains
one of the best books on the subject. Isaksson
was the first person to show that members of
the Qumran sect did marry like all other Jews,

but then they divorced their wives after they had fulfilled the command to have children.

On the Interpretation of the Gospel Texts

Allison, Dale, Jr. *Matthew.* 3 vols. International Critical Commentary. Edinburgh: T & T Clark, 1988-1997. For obscure scholarly details, you can't beat this commentary on Matthew.

Carson, Don. Matthew. In *Expositor's Bible Commentary.* Vol. 8. Grand Rapids: Zondervan, 1984. One of the best commentaries on Matthew.

Instone-Brewer, David. *Divorce and Remarriage in the Bible.* Grand Rapids: Eerdmans, 2002. Chapter 6, "Jesus' Teaching," goes through the Gospel texts in much more detail.

On Jesus' Teaching Against Polygamy

Instone-Brewer, David. "Jesus' Old Testament Basis for Monogamy." In *The Old Testament in the New Testament: Essays in Honour of J.L. North,* ed. Steve Moyise, JNTS Supp. 189. Sheffield, U.K.: Sheffield Academic Press, 2000.

See this article for academic details on this teaching.

6

WHEN YOUR PARTNER WALKS OUT

Christians shouldn't cause divorce, but sometimes they have to accept it.

Most of Paul's teaching on marriage and divorce is found in his first letter to the Corinthian church, written about A.D.55. Corinth was a major cosmopolitan city and was largely made up of Gentiles, though there were also a lot of Jews in the city and in the young church. They were having problems applying Jesus' teaching in a city that followed the Roman legal system. To complicate things further, Corinth was in the grip of a terrible famine, which made any kind of family life difficult.

PAUL DID NOT DISAPPROVE OF MARRIAGE

It is almost certain that Paul had been married when he was younger, though we know that he was single when he wrote 1 Corinthians. Marriage was compulsory for a pious Jew, and Paul said that before his conversion he was a very religious Pharisee (Acts 23:6; Phil 3:5). Every Jewish male was expected to marry in order to fulfill God's command to "multiply and fill the earth" (Gen 1:28); it was unthinkable that a pious young man would remain single. Paul's wife had probably died in childbirth (as happened all too often in the first century). We can surmise that he knew about marriage personally—its joys, responsibilities and sadnesses.

As well as being compulsory for Jews, marriage was compulsory in Roman law, though it was rarely enforced. This law had been enacted by the emperor Augustus, who saw that most Roman young men avoided marriage and fatherhood so that they could enjoy an endless series of affairs. He was worried by the lack of legal sons born into Roman households and by the weakening of the family unit, so in 18B.C. he introduced laws that made it compulsory to get married.

Paul contradicted both the Jewish and the Roman laws by teaching in 1 Corinthians 7 that marriage is optional. Corinth, being a Roman city, followed Roman law, and many members of its church were former Jews, so they also knew about Jewish law. Paul therefore had a tough job to convince them that, if they were not already married, they should not get married—at least, not yet.

Many people think this teaching means that Paul was against marriage, but he was only telling the Corinthians to wait until "the present distress" (1 Cor 7:26) was over. He did not need to tell them what kind of distress this was, because their suffering was all too obvious to them. Historians guess that he must have been referring to the famine that was afflicting the region at that time. In the first century, getting married meant having children, and it is not easy to care for babies and toddlers in a time of famine.

A QUESTION ABOUT SEX

In general Paul approved of marriage, but there were some Christians in Corinth who *were* against marriage and who wrote to Paul to ask him if he agreed. Paul quotes a phrase from their letter that encapsulates their viewpoint: "Now concerning the matters about which you wrote: 'It is good for a man not to have sexual relations with a woman'" (1 Cor 7:1).

One English translation unfortunately says, "Now for the matters you wrote about: It is good for a man not to marry," so that it looks as if Paul is making this statement himself and that he is against marriage. These are actually the words of some Corinthians who wanted to avoid sex. They thought that they could live holier lives if they avoided women, and one woman had evidently already left her husband (1 Cor 7:10-11).

Paul replies by reminding the Corinthian Christians what their marriage vows are. They promise to feed, clothe and share conjugal love with their spouse, and Paul emphasizes that if they neglect conjugal love they are "depriving" their partner.

> The husband should give to his wife her conjugal rights, and likewise the wife to her husband. For the wife does not have authority over her own body, but the husband does. Likewise the husband does not have authority over his own body, but the wife does. Do not deprive one another. (1 Cor 7:3-4)

Notice that Paul does not say that either partner can *demand* sexual love, because both should regard the other person as ruling over their body. Love is a matter not of taking but of *giving.* Paul is almost using the language of slavery, saying that they should both consider themselves to belong to the other. He has probably been influenced here by the context of the verse on which the marriage vows were based—the law about the rights of the slave wife in Exodus 21:10-11. Also, Paul does not define what this love consists of, because in some situations, a cuddle is a warmer expression of conjugal love than intercourse. Paul says that each should be concerned for the needs and wishes of their partner and not for themselves.

The couple could, of course, take a break from sexual relations, and Paul recognizes that this is sometimes a good thing if it makes extra time for prayer. But he also warns them that this should not be done for long, in case their abstinence led to sin: "Do not deprive one another, except perhaps by agreement for a limited time, that you may devote yourselves to prayer; but then come together again, so that Satan may not tempt you because of your lack of self-control" (1 Cor 7:5).

This is very similar to the type of rules that the rabbis made about conjugal rights. The rabbis also allowed such breaks and defined exactly how long they could be. For instance, you were allowed a longer break if your work took you away from home, and an even longer break if you were a rabbi, but you got no break at all if you were unemployed. Paul does not make legalistic definitions like these but just says that a couple may take a short break for prayer.

CARING FOR EACH OTHER

Paul reminds the Corinthians about their marriage vows by using language and ideas that would have been familiar to them from their Jewish background. Non-Jews would have found these concepts familiar as well, because Greek marriage contracts of the time also spoke of providing food and clothing, though most of them avoided mentioning conjugal love.

With regard to the vows to feed and clothe each other, Paul summarizes these obligations in a single category that we might call "material support." Similarly, the rabbis had various regulations concerning the neglect of physical affection and of material support. They defined exactly how much the man had to spend on food and cloth and how much cooking and sewing the woman had to do. Paul, however, does not specify quantities and simply says that spouses must "please" each other.

I want you to be free from anxieties. The unmarried man is anxious about the things of the Lord, how to please the Lord. But the married man is anxious about worldly things, how to please his wife, and his interests are divided. And the unmarried or betrothed woman is anxious about the things of the Lord, how to be holy in body and spirit. But the married woman is anxious about worldly things, how to please her husband. (1 Cor 7:32-34)

Paul sounds rather negative about marriage here, but as noted earlier, this was probably due to the famine. It was a difficult time to be married because it was difficult to keep the vows to provide food and clothes and general material care for each other, yet Scripture said that if a husband or wife willfully failed to provide food and clothing, they were guilty of neglect. Although Scripture did not specifically mention abuse, this was implied in the law against neglect. If a husband was not allowed to starve his wife or refuse her money for clothes, then he certainly could not beat his wife or rape or imprison her. Similarly, if a wife could not refuse to cook or sew for her husband, she certainly could not beat or poison or torture him.

ROMAN DIVORCE WAS TOO EASY

If anyone *did* do any of these things, there was an easy remedy: their partner could divorce them immediately and without any difficulty using Roman divorce-by-separation. This was possible because Corinth was run under Roman law, and even Jews could choose to use a Roman divorce if they wished. This Roman divorce was very easy—all you had to do was walk out of the house if your partner owned it, or tell your partner to get packing and leave the house if you owned it. There was no need to cite any grounds for ending the marriage, and having separated, you were both legally divorced and free to remarry.

For a victim of an abusive marriage, it was good that under Roman law they could get away from their partner without too much difficulty since they did not have to prove the abuse in court. But the problem was that divorce in Corinth was *too* easy: you did not need any good reason to get divorced, or, in fact, any reason at all. You could walk out on an innocent and loving partner, or you could even throw them out of the house if you owned it. Either partner could decide at any time to end the marriage, and the other partner became a helpless victim of this whim.

Even Christians in Corinth were using the Roman method of divorce-by-separation. Having separated from their partners they considered themselves divorced and free to remarry, and under Roman law they were. Paul had to remind them of the law of the Old Testament, pointing out that biblical divorce was always based on the grounds of broken vows, unlike the Roman groundless divorce. Therefore Christians should not practice the Roman divorce-by-separation—they should not simply separate from their partner and consider themselves legally divorced. "To the married I give this charge (not I, but the Lord): the wife should not separate from her husband (but if she does, she should remain unmarried or else be reconciled to her husband), and the husband should not dismiss his wife" (1 Cor 7:10).[1]

TRANSLATING "SEPARATE"

These verses are translated in various ways in different Bibles, but it is important to translate them as literally as possible, especially concerning the way in which the separation occurs. Paul pictures both the husband and the wife deciding for themselves to divorce. She "separates herself" (that is, she walks out on him); he decides to "dismiss his wife" (that is, send her packing). The differences lie in the fact that the husband was the one most likely to own the house, so for the wife to divorce her husband she would have to leave the house (that is, "separate herself"), while for the husband to divorce his wife he would have to tell her to leave his house (that is, "dismiss her"). In this situation Paul is not talking to partners who were divorced against their will, since both the man and the woman in these verses make their own decision to separate from their partner.

If you want the technical details of the translation, here they are, but you can ignore them and skip ahead if you prefer: Paul uses *separate* in the reflexive mood, i.e., "separate themselves," but this Greek form is exactly like the passive mood, "be separated." This has confused a lot of translators, but in 1 Corinthians 7:15 Paul uses the same word again, with exactly the same form, in a context where it cannot possibly be passive and *must* be reflexive: "If the unbelieving partner separates, let it be so." In effect he is saying, if an unbeliever leaves a believer, let them do so, because after all there is very little the believer can do about it. Now, if "separate" were translated in verse 15 with the passive rather than the reflexive, it would be: "If the unbelieving partner is separated, let it be so"—in other words, any believer can leave an unbelieving spouse, and if they do, we should do nothing about it and just let it happen. This is patently the wrong translation, because it is exactly the opposite of what Paul had already said in 1 Corinthians 7:10-11. Therefore the correct translation is "separate themselves."

To leave the technicalities behind: Paul's point is that Christians should not use this Roman form of divorce-by-separation because it is groundless, therefore it is too easy to divorce people against their will when they have done nothing wrong. Anybody could take it on themselves to separate, and their partner would suddenly find that they had been legally divorced whether they wanted it or not. For Christians, this is simply not an option.

WHAT IF YOU HAVE USED DIVORCE-BY-SEPARATION?

But some Christians had *already* used divorce-by-separation, and Paul was keen to tell them what to do in that situation. "If she does [separate herself], she should remain unmarried or else be reconciled to her husband" (1 Cor 7:11). He is saying that if someone has separated, they should not consider themselves to be divorced but should try to reverse the separation by remaining unmarried while trying to be reconciled again. In other words, they should do all that they can to reverse the Roman divorce-by-separation.

Paul was probably thinking of a particular woman at this point because he says "she," but in the rest of this chapter he was always careful to address both men and women, even to the point of repeating himself in an almost tiresome way. The Corinthians presumably knew which woman Paul was referring to, but we can only guess the reason she separated from her husband. The only clue we have is in 1 Corinthians 7:1, where Paul quotes the Corinthians' letter asking him about the teaching of some groups that taught that holiness included avoiding sex: "It is good for a man not to have sexual relations with a woman" (and vice versa). The woman was probably influenced by one such group, but as we saw above, Paul certainly did not regard this as a biblical reason for divorce.

Paul points out that Jesus himself condemned this type of groundless divorce, because he rejected the Jewish groundless divorce (the "Any Cause" divorce). The only difference in the Roman groundless divorce was that women as well as men could initiate it. Paul assumed that if Jesus condemned the Jewish groundless divorce, then he would condemn the Roman one. This is why Paul tells the Christians that the Lord commands them not to separate (1 Cor 7:10).

WHAT IF YOU ARE A VICTIM OF DIVORCE-BY-SEPARATION?

What about the *victim* of a divorce-by-separation? Paul has told the person who enacted the separation that they should remain unmarried and try to effect a reconciliation, but what if you have been forced into a divorce by your partner even though you did not want to split up? Paul addresses this situation in 1 Corinthians 7:15: "But if the unbelieving partner separates, let it be so. In such cases the brother or sister is not enslaved. God has called you to peace."[2]

In effect, he says that if a non-Christian divorces you, you should let him or her go. This seems like a sudden U-turn—as if Paul does not care and as though he does not want marriages between Christians and non-Christians to last. But we know this is not true, since he said the opposite in 1 Corinthians 7:12-13, where he tells Christians not to divorce their non-Christian partner: "If any brother has a wife who is an unbeliever, and she consents to live with him, he should not dismiss her. If any woman has a husband who is an unbeliever, and he consents to live with her, she should not dismiss him."[3]

So Paul does not want Christians to divorce their non-Christian partners, and yet he says that Christians should let non-Christians divorce them. This does not seem to make sense until we look at it pragmatically. Ask yourself, what can the divorced Christian partner do? Their non-Christian husband or wife has told them the marriage is over; the husband has dismissed his wife or the wife has walked out. What can Paul tell the Christian to do to reverse this divorce? Of course, they should have been doing their utmost to hold the marriage together before the divorce, but once it has happened, any attempts at reconciliation are unlikely to work and are likely to be seen as pestering.

Paul teaches that once such a divorce has happened, a line should be drawn under it; he says, in effect, "If they divorce you, there is not much you can do; if the actual divorce-by-separation has happened, then let them go." He then adds that God has called us to peace and not to endless conflict after a divorce.

CONCLUSION: DIVORCE SHOULD BE THE LAST OPTION

Paul and Jesus have the same message for two different cultures:

1. Believers should never cause a divorce—that is, they should not break their marriage vows.

2. Believers should not use a groundless divorce—Jewish believers should not use the Hillelite "Any Cause" divorce, and no one should use the Roman "divorce-by-separation."

Jesus adds that believers should do all they can to save a marriage, which includes forgiving a partner who breaks vows and then repents. And Paul adds that believers who have wrongly enacted a divorce-by-separation should attempt to be reconciled and not remarry because that would make the divorce irreversible.

Paul says further that if someone is divorced against their will, they may accept it. There is nothing they can do to reverse the divorce, and God has called them to peace.

But this leaves us with two questions:

116

- Can a believer divorce a partner who breaks their vows unrepentantly?

- And can a believer remarry after a divorce?

These questions will be answered in following chapters, but first we have to ask a more fundamental question: Do marriages *ever* end in the sight of God?

FURTHER READING

On Roman Divorce Law

The following are a couple of good introductions to Roman divorce law:

Rabello, Afredo M. "Divorce of Jews in the Roman Empire." In *The Jewish Law Annual,* ed. B.S. Jackson, 4:79-102. Leiden, Boston: E.J. Brill, 1981.

Treggiari, Susan. "Divorce Roman Style: How Easy and How Frequent Was It?" In *Marriage, Divorce and Children in Ancient Rome,* ed. Beryl Rawson, pp.31-46. Oxford: Clarendon, 1991.

On Greco-Roman Divorce Vocabulary

Instone-Brewer, David. "1 Corinthians 7 in the Light of the Graeco-Roman Marriage and Divorce Papyri." *Tyndale Bulletin* 52 (2001):101-16. In this article I analyze Greco-Roman legal texts from the first century.

_____, ed. *Marriage and Divorce Papyri of the Ancient Greek, Roman and Jewish World.* 2000. www.Tyndale.cam.ac.uk/Brewer/MarriagePapyri. The basis for the previous article: a collection of all the divorce and marriage documents in Greek and Latin from the first century and surrounding centuries.

On Interpreting 1 Corinthians 7

Fee, Gordon. *The First Epistle to the Corinthians.* New International Commentary on the New Testament. Grand Rapids: Eerdmans, 1987. The best commentary on this epistle.

Instone-Brewer, David. *Divorce and Remarriage in the Bible.* Grand Rapids: Eerdmans, 2002. Chapter 7, "Paul's Teaching," deals with 1 Corinthians 7 in much more detail.

7

TILL DEATH US DO PART?

Is a divorcee still married in God's eyes?

What is in the middle of both America and Australia? Answer: The letter *r*.

Another riddle: If a woman is born in Italy, marries in England, moves to America and dies in Baltimore, what is she?

I must admit that when I first heard this I did not get it at all. Several possibilities came to mind: What is the first letter of each place? *I, E, A, B.* Or what shape did her journey make? Or what is at the first letter of the place where she was born and the last letter of the place where she died? But I was on completely the wrong track because I ignored the obvious—a woman born in Italy, married in England, moved to and died in America, what is she? Answer: dead!

All right, here is another seemingly simple riddle with a catch: A woman falls in love, gets engaged and gets married. Her husband commits adultery, moves in with his mistress and divorces her. What is her marital status?

The obvious answer is "single" or "divorced." But many Bible scholars would say, "Married—because only death can end a marriage."

LIFE-LONG MARRIAGE CAN BE A CURSE

Is death the only end to marriage? If it were, some people would regard this as a blessing from God because it represents a lifetime guarantee on their marriage. But others, who have found that the person they married is actually unfaithful or violent, would see it as a life sentence of imprisonment with a most cruel enemy.

Few things last forever, or even for a lifetime, and this is what makes marriage such a special event in one's life. Someone has proposed to you, saying, "I love you and only you," and at the wedding they say, "I will love you, honor you and keep you through poverty and illness, till death us do part." Is there anything more affirming than for someone you love to make this life-long commitment to you? That is why it is so devastating when those vows are broken. But it happens.

People commit adultery or become cruel or abusive, and their marriages start to break down. What happens then? Most marriages can be healed with effort from both partners, but like cancer, if it is left untreated too long, broken vows are terminal because they kill a marriage.

When a marriage has reached this condition, a Christian can do one of three things:

1. remain together and suffer, in the hope that things will get better

2. separate without getting divorced

3. get divorced

But should a Christian ever get divorced? Doesn't marriage last forever?

Some Christians say "Once married, always married." I would love to say that this is true and that all marriages can be saved—that God blesses each marriage and keeps it together whatever happens. But I have some bad news for you. Some marriages cannot be rescued, and the Bible does not promise that all marriages have a lifetime guarantee.

TEXTS THAT MIGHT IMPLY LIFE-LONG MARRIAGE

It's true that a few texts in the Bible do seem to say that only death can end a marriage, but this is only when the context or the actual words used are ignored. One example of this is the saying "Those whom God has joined, no one can separate." As we saw in the first chapter, what the text actually says is "let no one separate"—which implies that marriage can end, though this is very undesirable.

There are three other New Testament texts that appear to say that all marriages last for a lifetime, and two that seem to say that only death can end a marriage. The rest of this chapter is going to examine these texts in their context. You may be tempted to skip this chapter, but please don't, because it is central for understanding the biblical basis of remarriage.

The first text is Jesus' description of remarriage after divorce as "adultery" (Mt 19:9 and parallels), which implies that a divorcee is still married. However, as we saw in chapter five, Jesus was specifically referring to the new "Any

Cause" divorces rather than all types of divorce. He condemned the "Any Cause" divorces as unbiblical and invalid—and said that if you get remarried after an invalid divorce, you are technically committing adultery. So rather than saying in this text that marriage lasts a lifetime, in context Jesus is simply emphasizing that the "Any Cause" divorce was not a valid one.

The second way in which Scripture appears to support the "marriage lasts a lifetime" teaching is the description of a married couple as "one flesh," which seems to imply a permanent condition that can only end with death (Mt 19:5-6 and parallels). It sounds as if in marriage two people have permanently become a new individual. This is, of course, what *should* happen, and it is sad that it's not always how things turn out.

Paul points out that, sadly, people can become "one flesh" with prostitutes (1 Cor 6:15-20) and says that this is a very serious sin because Christians are a temple of the Holy Spirit. But he does not say that a "one flesh" relationship with a prostitute is permanent. If it were, he would have had to warn those at Corinth who were converted fornicators (1 Cor 6:11) that they must remain single because their previous one-flesh relationships prohibited them from getting married. Paul certainly regarded a one-flesh relationship as more intimate than any other, but he did not think that it was, by definition, a permanent relationship. So although the phrase describes a relationship that should be lifelong, it does not guarantee that the relationship *will* last for a lifetime.

The last text that appears to imply that marriage is always life-long is Ephesians 5:32. In the original Greek, Christ's marriage to the church is described as a "mystery" (Greek *musterion*), but when the Greek was translated into Latin, the word *musterion* or "mystery" was translated as "sacrament" (Latin *sacramentum*). This was a perfectly good translation in the fourth century because *sacramentum* meant "a secret, hidden in holiness," but over subsequent centuries the meaning of *sacrament* started to change. By medieval times it had come to mean "an unchangeable sacred reality," such as the Sacrament of the Priesthood, which refers to a permanent transformation of a layperson into a priest when he makes his vows before the bishop. Similarly, "the Sacrament of Marriage" refers to the permanent transformation of two individuals into a married couple when they make their vows before a priest.

Whether or not you agree with the theology of sacraments, there is no biblical basis for saying that marriage is a sacrament, except for the Latin Vulgate translation of Ephesians 5:32, which was made when *sacrament* meant something similar to "mystery."

These suggestions that marriage is always life-long turn out to have no biblical foundation, but we must still examine two important texts that both appear to say that only death can end a marriage. These two texts (in 1 Cor 7 and Rom 7) are actually more important for what they do not say, because although they both say that death can end a marriage, neither of them mentions divorce. Using them to draw conclusions about divorce, then, is a type of reasoning called "an argument from silence." Before we examine these texts, we have to know how to decide when an argument from silence is relevant and when the silence is merely coincidental.

WHEN SILENCE SPEAKS VOLUMES

An argument from silence depends on the assumption that a particular silence is very significant. But how can you tell if the silence is deliberate or incidental? Sometimes a silence is the key to understanding a passage, but at other times it is no more significant than neglecting to say "I love you" at the end of a phone call—and drawing conclusions from this type of silence can lead to huge misunderstandings!

Jesus uses silence in a very significant way with the rich young ruler (Mt 19:16-22; Lk 18:18-23). The first four of the Ten Commandments deal with God, and the last six deal with humankind, and when Jesus asks the young man if he has kept the commandments, Jesus lists commandments from the second section—he is interested in how this ruler interacts with humanity. Actually Jesus lists only commandments five through nine and then falls silent, omitting number ten. The rich young ruler ignores the silence and says he has obeyed them all. But of course Jesus had been *deliberately* silent about that last commandment, which is "You shall not covet"—that is, do not long for what others own. Jesus knows that this is where the young man's difficulty lies, and he proves it by asking him to do something that he never asked of anyone else: to give away all his wealth. Jesus knows the rich young ruler can't do it because his besetting sin is covetousness. Instead of asking for help with that sin, the man goes away sad.

But there are other times when it is very difficult to know if a silence is significant. Have you noticed that the New Testament never talks about musical instruments in the church? Old Testament believers used all kinds of instruments to worship God; this is apparent especially in the Psalms. But in the New Testament, instruments are mentioned only in reference to non-Christian worship and in reference to heaven. Ephesians says that Christians worship with "psalms and hymns and spiritual songs" (Eph 5:19), but it does not mention instruments. Because of this omission, many Christian groups used to reject all instruments; their worship was led with voices only, in order to be faithful to Scripture. The introduction of the organ and other musical instruments is a relatively modern innovation that several Christian leaders resisted because of the New Testament's silence about musical instruments. One denomination still follows the "noninstrumental" tradition.

There is one silence in Scripture that inspired the start of a whole new sect. Right at the start of Genesis, in the story of the creation of Eve, it says that God put Adam to sleep, but it does not say anywhere that God woke him up. If this silence is significant, it implies that Adam is still asleep now, so everything that has happened since then is part of Adam's dream! Mary Baker Eddy noticed this and founded the Christian Scientists. She said that since we are living in Adam's dream, our illnesses are merely illusions, and as soon as we realize the truth, those illnesses and other problems will evaporate.

How can we tell if a silence in Scripture is significant or not? The best way is to ask ourselves: Is the silence surprising? Would the original reader or hearer say to themselves: *How strange—he missed that?* When Jesus omits one of the Ten Commandments, it is obvious and startling, but when the New Testament neglects to mention Jesus' ever going to the bathroom, it is just that there were more important things to say.[1] It is no more significant than the fact that all the references to toilets are in the Old Testament. Perhaps a new denomination will arise that will refuse to build toilets on church property!

ROMANS 7: 2: THE CHURCH AS CHRIST'S BRIDE

Now we come to the silence about divorce in these two texts, and we have to ask in both cases whether the silence is surprising and significant—whether the absence of divorce in these texts imply that marriage cannot end through divorce. We will find that the silence is not at all un-expected in these texts, because the context rules out any mention of ending a marriage through divorce.

The first text is Romans 7:2, which we have to read in its context:

> Do you not know, brothers—for I am speaking to those who know the law—that the Law is binding on a person only as long as he lives? Thus a married woman is bound by law to her husband while he lives, but if her husband dies she is released from the law of marriage. Accordingly, she will be called an adulteress if she lives with another man while her husband is alive. But if her husband dies, she is free from that law, and if she marries another man she is not an adulteress. Likewise, my brothers, you also

have died to the Law through the body of Christ, so that you may belong to another, to him who has been raised from the dead, in order that we may bear fruit for God. (Rom 7:1-4)

This can be summarized thus: People are tied to the law of Moses till they die, just as a wife is tied to her husband till death. If she went with another man this would be adultery, unless her husband had died. Therefore God lets you die with Christ, in order to set you free to marry Christ.

Paul compares our relationship to the law to that of a woman's relationship to her husband. A Jewish believer is like someone who is married to the law—a demanding perfectionist who can never be pleased. This believer meets Christ and falls in love with him, but she cannot marry him because if she did she would be committing adultery. All she can do is wait until the marriage ends through death—although, of course, her husband, the law, is eternal and so her wait is hopeless. But the wonderful news that Paul brings is that Christ died for her, and she has died with Christ. Therefore her marriage to the law *has* ended through death—her death—and now she is free to marry Christ!

This is a wonderful picture of Christ's love, whose death frees us from the law. The passage tells us a great deal about our salvation, but we should not expect it to teach us about divorce and remarriage. Just as the parable of the sower is not a good manual for teaching us about farming, so we should not expect to learn much about marriage from an illustration about a believer's marriage to the law and to Christ.

Nevertheless, the woman in this picture thinks her marriage can end only through death, so this might seem to imply that it cannot end through divorce or through desertion. But how *could* her marriage to the law end in these ways? The law would never desert her or break his marriage vows in any way that would lead to divorce, because, being the law, he would always keep them *to the letter!* So the whole concept of divorce or desertion would be out of place in this picture, and no reader would expect Paul to mention them or be surprised at their absence. In fact it would be astonishing if divorce or desertion *were* mentioned, because it would make the illustration break down.

1 CORINTHIANS 7: 39: WIDOWS' FREEDOM TO REMARRY

The other text that fails to mention divorce is 1 Corinthians 7:39. The first half of chapter 7 is addressed to those who are married (1 Cor 7:1-17), and in the second half (1 Cor 7:25-40) Paul talks to various types of unmarried people, including virgins, those "released" from marriage and those promised in marriage, and finally those who are widowed. "A wife is bound to her husband as long as he lives. But if her husband dies, she is free to be married to whom she wishes, only in the Lord" (1 Cor 7:39).

Since he is addressing people whose marriages have ended because of the death of their partner, we should not be surprised that Paul does not mention divorce; it would be completely out of place in this context. Here too it is wrong to think that the text implies that marriage always lasts until death, because the reason for the silence about divorce is simply that it would not have been mentioned in this context.

The reason Paul says this to the widows is in order to free them from the Old Testament law of levirate marriage (Deut 25:5-10), which many Jews still imposed on widows. According to this law, a widow without a son had to marry her brother-in-law to ensure there was a male to inherit the family land in Israel. However, by the first century, most families had long ago sold their land or lost it permanently, or lived outside the land of Israel, so the levirate law no longer made sense, and many Jewish leaders were beginning to ignore it. They saw that it had become nothing more than an unnecessary burden on widows, who felt forced into a loveless marriage with a brother-in-law. Paul was the first Jew (as far as we know) to explicitly say that this law should no longer apply. He told all widows: You may marry whoever you like—that is, you do not have to marry your brother-in-law if you do not want to.

TO CONCLUDE: CASE NOT PROVED

We have come to the end of this chapter having learned what seems to be a very negative message. We have failed to find any evidence that God gives a lifetime guarantee with every marriage. Although some people may be disappointed by this, there will be others—those who are suffering cruel abuse or who have been deserted—who may be relieved to hear that God does not imprison them in a marriage when their partner has so obviously and painfully broken it up.

We have learned that God is not constrained by any supposed universal law that marriage lasts a lifetime, and we have found nothing in the Bible that speaks about any such rule. Instead, we find that

- Jesus commands those who have been joined through marriage vows that they *should* never separate, but a sinner who disregards Jesus' command can still break up the marriage.

- The phrase "one flesh" describes a very real unity that married partners find in sexual union, but it is not necessarily permanent—for instance, when that union is with a prostitute.

- Although marriage is as special as any sacrament, this does not guarantee that it will last forever; marriages *don't* always last until death.

- The fact that divorce is absent from two texts does not mean that this silence is significant, especially when divorce would not fit in the context—as is the case with the two texts that are usually cited.

We have found no reason to believe that God changed his mind about divorce between the Old Testament and the New Testament. In both Testaments God is on the side of the victim of marriage breakup and allows the victim to divorce a partner who is unfaithful, neglectful or abusive.

We do also have a positive conclusion—that God understands us. He lovingly provides a way out of an impossible situation rather than inflexibly and legalistically ruling that all mar-riages must continue until death, regardless of how faithless or abusive your partner is to you. God abhors the sin of broken marriage vows, but he knows our limitations and wants to deal with our sinfulness. He sees what people suffer in secret and gives comfort and a practical solution to the victim. Divorce does not take away the hurt, but it does not perpet-uate it either. Even if the victim of a marriage breakup cannot find love elsewhere, they can at least find peace, and they can feel safe in the knowledge that the one who betrayed their love no longer has any claim on their life.

These conclusions leave us asking a question: If divorce is possible, *when* is it possible? We will look at this in the next chapter.

FURTHER READING

Bible Teaching About Life-long Marriage

Atkinson, David. *To Have and to Hold: The Marriage Covenant and the Discipline of Divorce.* London: Collins, 1979. Atkinson provides a good historical overview of how this doctrine arose.

Cornes, Andrew. *Divorce and Remarriage: Biblical Principles and Pastoral Practice.* London: Hodder & Stoughton, 1993. The best account that disagrees with mine.

On Interpreting the "Difficult" Texts

Little, Joyce A. "Paul's Use of Analogy: A Structural Analysis of Romans 7.1-6." *Catholic Biblical Quarterly* 46 (1984):82-90. Includes an extremely detailed analysis of Romans 7:2.

Olsen, V. Norskov. *The New Testament Logia on Divorce: A Study of Their Interpretation from Erasmus to Milton.* Tübingen: Mohr-Siebeck, 1971. Erasmus was the first person to interpret these texts in the light of their context, and other Reformers followed him. This history is dealt with well in Olsen's work.

8

FOUR BIBLICAL GROUNDS FOR DIVORCE

These include abuse and neglect.

Someone e-mailed me the following story:

> I was the adult Sunday school teacher in a Baptist church, and my pastor invited me to sit with the deacons and himself in a difficult decision. A young lady had been constantly threatened by her alcoholic husband. One afternoon, he came to her with a shotgun while she was visiting her sister. After chasing her out into a field, he pinned her down, put the shotgun to her head and pulled the trigger, but the gun jammed. He served a few months in the county jail. My pastor explained that our church took a hard and fast view that divorce was always sin, so if we followed that we would be advising her to reconcile with her husband once he was released from jail. As I pondered that, I could not believe that God could possibly ask her to do that, and I said so. The decision that was eventually

made was that she could separate from him, but not divorce, and was to live the rest of her life in that state unless he died. I felt this was better for her than reconciliation, but I didn't have complete peace with that either.

Although this is an extreme example, any Christian counselor will tell you that abuse within marriage is very common, and there are a huge number of people who live in fear in their own homes. The husband or wife who is the victim of physical abuse or emotional torture by their partner lives as if they were imprisoned in a double cell with their worst enemy. As much as we would like to believe otherwise, it happens within Christian marriages as well, although it is difficult to tell exactly how frequently, because those involved are often too ashamed or embarrassed to admit it even to a friend or relative.

THE CHURCH STRUGGLES TO BE JUST

The church has struggled with its handling of these situations for centuries. Origen, the greatest of the church fathers at the start of the third century, faced the issue squarely in his commentary on Matthew.[1] He asked why

Jesus did not allow a husband to divorce a wife who had tried to poison him or who had killed one of their children, because "to endure sins of such heinousness which seem to be worse than adultery or fornication, will appear to be irrational." Even though he did not understand how it could possibly be right or just, Origen concluded that we should nevertheless obey Jesus' teaching because it would be "impious" to do otherwise.

In modern times most Christian teachers would likewise say, "I know it sounds harsh, but unless your believing partner has committed adultery, the New Testament is clear that you must stay with him or her and trust God who has bound you together." Andrew Cornes, who wrote an excellent book in support of this traditional church teaching (*Divorce and Remarriage: Biblical Principles and Pastoral Practice),* makes one concession: he says that if your life is at risk because of the amount of abuse you are suffering, then you are allowed to *separate,* though you may not divorce. Many others extend this concession to include all abusive marriages. We may well sympathize with this way of solving the problem—it does, after all, seem fairer for a victim of abuse to be allowed to separate even if they cannot divorce—but the solution is not biblical. A couple should not separate without getting divorced, because Paul specifically says that married couples may not separate (1 Cor 7:10-11). So if we take the traditional interpretation of the New Testament seriously, no one may separate from an abusing partner.

We have already seen that God gave clear and fair laws in the Old Testament to limit the damage caused by the sin of neglect and abuse: the victim was allowed to decide whether or not they wanted the marriage to end. Would God really have abandoned this wise and practical approach in New Testament times or is it a principle for the church today? In this chapter we will find that neither Jesus nor Paul abrogates these Old Testament principles and that Paul assumes that they are still in force.

WHY WAS JESUS SILENT ABOUT THE VICTIM'S RIGHT TO DIVORCE?

It seems surprising that Jesus should ignore this important ethical Old Testament principle on divorce, especially when he gave such serious warnings about neglecting even the smallest commandment. The occasion when the Pharisees asked him about their "Any Cause" divorce would have been a perfect time to say something because, as we saw in chapter five, Jesus took this opportunity to speak to them about many other aspects of marriage and divorce that they had not asked him about. He spoke about the ideal of life-long marriage, the facts that divorce was never compulsory and that marriage was not compulsory, about monogamy and, of course, about his interpretation of "a cause of sexual immorality"—that it means only sexual immorality and not also "Any Cause."[2] So if Jesus believed that neglect and abuse were valid grounds for divorce, why didn't he say something about them?

The most likely answer is that he did not need to say anything—or he *did* say something but the Gospel writers did not think it was necessary to record it—because the principle was so universally accepted that there was no dispute about it. There are several other universally accepted truths that Jesus did not teach anywhere, such as the doctrine that there is only one God. The oneness of God was agreed on by everyone, so there was no need for Jesus to teach it. He was also silent about rape and manslaughter, but this does not mean that he was unconcerned about victims of these crimes.

The matters on which Jesus *did* speak out—that marriage is not compulsory, that divorce is not compulsory after adultery, that neither polygamy nor divorce for "Any Cause" is acceptable—were those on which his teaching was against the teaching of either all or some first-century Jews. There were no debates about the validity of neglect and abuse as grounds for divorce in any ancient Jewish literature, for the same reason that there are none about the oneness of God: these principles were unanimously agreed on. Rather than indicating that Jesus did not accept the validity of divorce for neglect and abuse, his silence about it highlights the fact that he did accept it, like all other Jews at that time.

DIDN'T JESUS ALLOW ONLY ONE GROUND FOR DIVORCE?

If it is the case that Jesus did accept other valid grounds, how do we reconcile that with his statement that there was only *one* valid ground for divorce, when he said (in Mt 19:9 and par.) there was no divorce "except for 'sexual immorality'"?

Although it does initially sound like a contradiction, it is only so if Jesus meant that adultery was the only valid ground for divorce in *Scrip-*

ture, whereas the Gospels imply that he meant adultery was the only valid ground that is found in Deuteronomy 24:1. As we saw in chapter five, the Gospels record the whole debate as if it was concerned solely with divorces in Deuteronomy 24:1.

The Pharisees open the debate by asking, "Is it lawful to divorce one's wife for 'Any Cause'?" which is a direct reference to the controversial phrase in Deuteronomy 24:1, "a cause of sexual immorality." Also the Pharisees' phrasing, "Is it lawful to divorce *one's wife...?*"[3] implies that they are concerned with divorces that can be initiated only by a man. Since the types of divorce in Exodus 21 could be initiated by both men and women, the question demonstrates that they are specifically concerned with the types of divorce in Deuteronomy 24:1, which can be initiated only by a man.

As we saw in chapter five, Jesus ignores the question at first and speaks instead about marriage—which he considers more important than divorce—but the Pharisees again try to restrict the debate to Deuteronomy 24:1 by reminding Jesus about the "certificate of divorce." All the Old Testament teaching on this is in Deuteronomy 24:1; it is not mentioned in Exodus 21 or anywhere else in the law of

Moses. All this shows that the only thing the Pharisees want is a straight answer from Jesus about his interpretation of "a cause of sexual immorality" in Deuteronomy 24:1.

Jesus gives them their answer, and it is one that they recognize immediately because it was the same as that of the Shammaite Pharisees, who said that there is no valid divorce in Deuteronomy 24:1 "except for 'sexual immorality.'" That is, a divorce for sexual immorality is valid, but a divorce for "Any Cause" is not.

When the Shammaites said there was no divorce "except for 'sexual immorality,'" they did not mean that they rejected the validity of other biblical grounds for divorce. We know this because we have records of debates they had with the Hillelites about these grounds—the neglect of food and clothing. These debates were not about whether or not divorce for neglect was valid—that was accepted; they were about how to *define* neglect. They debated the minimum quantities of food and clothing that had to be provided and the amount of "conjugal love" that was necessary to avoid being charged with neglecting one's partner.

It is somewhat surprising to find out from the Talmud that some rabbis a century or so later thought that the early Shammaites did reject all grounds for divorce in Scripture except for sexual immorality. These rabbis lived about two hundred years after the demise of the Shammaite cause, so perhaps their mistake is understandable. By that time all Jews followed Hillelite teaching, and they had long forgotten what the Shammaites had actually believed. They quoted the slogan "nothing except sexual immorality" thinking that it meant "this is the only type of divorce in the *whole of Scripture.*" They forgot that the original context of this Shammaite slogan was the debate about the types of divorce just in *Deuteronomy 24:1.*[4]

Christian interpreters have made exactly the same mistake with the words of Jesus. Like the later rabbis, they forgot (or did not realize) that the context of the phrase "nothing except 'sexual immorality'" was a question about the meaning of Deuteronomy 24:1. Jesus used exactly the same words as the Shammaites in exactly the same context (a debate about Deut 24:1) with exactly the same people (the Pharisees) in the same time and place (first-century Palestine), so we have to conclude that Jesus and the Shammaites meant the same thing—there is only one valid type of divorce in Deuteronomy 24:1. Neither he nor the Shammaites implied by this that there is only one valid type of divorce *in the whole of Scripture.*

We have concluded that Jesus' words in Matthew 19:9 (and par.) only exclude divorce for "Any Cause," but does this mean that Jesus accepted the grounds given in Exodus 21:10-11? As we saw earlier in this chapter, we can probably assume that he did accept them because if he had not he would have said so. This law in Exodus is not as self-evident to us as it was to first-century Jews so this conclusion is, perhaps, not so obvious to us. Fortunately Paul *does* specifically refer to this law.

PAUL TEACHES FOUR GROUNDS FOR DIVORCE

In 1 Corinthians 7 Paul refers to the three grounds for divorce in Exodus 21 when he replies to the Corinthians' question about leaving their partners (see chapter six): "If he takes another wife to himself, he shall not diminish her food, her clothing, or her conjugal love" (Ex 21:10).[5]

He reminds those who want to stop physical relations with their husband or wife that they had made a vow to share "conjugal love" with them (1 Cor 7:3-5). Later in the chapter, when he suggests that people should postpone their marriage plans because of the famine, he reminds them that marriage involves promising to clothe and feed their partner, which he summarizes as being "anxious about worldly things, how to please" each other (1 Cor 7:32-34).

Paul's readers would have immediately recognized his references to these grounds for divorce, even if they were not Jews, because they had also become the basis for Greek and Roman marriage and divorce law. This law spread throughout the whole known world via the Babylonian and then the Persian empires, to Greek culture and eventually to Roman law. These three grounds for divorce were written into both Jewish and Greco-Roman marriage documents. This meant that if you were suffering neglect from your husband or wife, you could present your case in any court—Roman, rabbinic, Egyptian or, as far as we know, any of the other provincial legal systems of the first-century civilized world.

Therefore, although Paul does not specifically say that these three areas of neglect can be grounds for divorce, the fact that he talks about them as obligations implies that he accepted them and agreed with them. The Scripture text from which they come (Ex 21:10-11) is primarily concerned with releasing the neglected person from the marriage; thus the three obligations are merely a secondary meaning inferred from the grounds for divorce in this text. If Paul did not accept these grounds for divorce, he would not have used these verses as a basis for his teaching on the obligations within marriage.

As well as these three grounds of divorce for neglect, Paul presumably also allowed divorce on the ground of adultery. Although he does not say so, most interpreters assume that he did allow this because Jesus allowed it. Another reason for believing that he allowed it was because, like these three grounds of neglect, adultery was universally recognized as a ground for divorce. Therefore, as with all the other biblical grounds for divorce, Paul would have had to state very clearly that he disagreed with it if he did not want believers to assume that he permitted divorces on these grounds.

Paul says virtually nothing about divorce itself; perhaps he deliberately avoided this subject because he wanted to present a more hopeful teaching. By emphasizing the obligations within marriage he was hoping that the need for divorces on these grounds would never arise. Certainly they never *should* arise, if believers obey this teaching. He was keen for Christians to avoid causing a marriage breakup, and so he stressed the four biblical *obligations in marriage* rather than the four biblical grounds for divorce.

However, Paul did not expect that unbelievers would necessarily follow this teaching. As we saw in chapter six, he tells believers that if they are abandoned by their unbelieving partners, they are "not enslaved" (1 Cor 7:15). As we will see in the next chapter, this phrase is a reference to divorce, and so Paul is telling believers that they can regard abandonment as a valid divorce. He does not say why, but it would have been obvious to any first-century reader—and is obvious to us now that we understand the principles of Exodus 21:10—that if they were a victim of desertion, they had the right to divorce on the grounds of neglect.

In summary, Paul accepts all four Old Testament grounds for divorce. He accepts unfaithfulness as a ground because this was allowed by Jesus (Deut 24:1), and he also accepts neglect of food, clothing and conjugal love (Ex 21:10-11).

DEFINING BIBLICAL GROUNDS FOR DIVORCE

How can we apply and define these four grounds for divorce in the twenty-first century?

The ground of unfaithfulness is of course easily understood, though it is too easy sometimes to condemn the adultery and ignore the neglect that caused the rift and eventually resulted in adultery. Although neglect by one partner does not excuse adultery by the other, it is important to realize that the fault is often not just one sided.

Provision of food and clothing is summarized by Paul as "caring for" or "pleasing" each other (1 Cor 7:32, 34). As we saw in chapter six, Paul does not define the amount of care to be provided (as the rabbis did) but says that we should aim to please each other, which means that he was more concerned with the motivation for caring than with legalistic details.

Provision of conjugal love is the most difficult of the marital obligations to define, especially if someone is using it as a ground for divorce. The rabbis went to the lengths of defining how many times a man had to make love to his wife, specifying different intervals for different occupations. Most men had to do their duty twice a week, though ass drivers only once a week (because they often went on trips for a few days to deliver goods), and those without work were expected to fulfill their obligation *every* night. There were no such rules for women, probably because the rabbis considered them to be rapacious individuals who were always pestering their husbands.

The rabbis were reluctant to allow a divorce on the ground of refusing conjugal activity; in such situations they tried to resolve the issue by talking to the offender or by applying gradually increasing fines. Therefore if a woman continually refused her husband, a rabbinic court could fine her by reducing her *ketubah* (marriage inheritance) a little each week, and if a man refused his wife then her *ketubah* could be increased a little each week.

We should also look for the principles that lie behind these requirements. A husband who never lets his wife buy makeup, medical supplies or occasional leisure items such as books or CDs has not, strictly speaking, neglected her food or clothing. Similarly, a man who makes love to his wife once a week but never shows her any other kind of affection could be said to fulfill his obligation to provide "conjugal love," but it would be very legalistic to say that he was fulfilling her needs. The principle behind "food and clothing" can be called "material support," and the principle behind "conjugal love" can be called "physical affection." When neglect becomes positive harm, it turns into abuse—neglect of material support becomes physical abuse, and neglect of physical affection turns into emotional abuse.

HOW CAN ONE DEFINE CONJUGAL LOVE?

Paul does not define the frequency of conjugal activity or suggest fines for withholding it as the rabbis did, but he tells both partners that they should regard conjugal love as if it were a debt that they owe to each other (1 Cor 7:3-5). Paul is careful not to say that anyone has the right to *demand* conjugal love, but he says that both partners owe this support, because love is something that we give and not something that we take.

The term *conjugal love* should not be defined as narrowly as "sexual intercourse," because this can become impractical or inappropriate in cases of illness or frailty. Physical affection can be demonstrated in many different ways; often a hug is far more appreciated than intercourse.

The most difficult question is how broadly we can extend the principle of physical affection. The Hebrew word for "love" in Exodus 21:10 (*'onah*) is very difficult to define because it occurs so rarely, but the most likely meaning is "conjugal love," which is how the ancient rabbis interpreted it. We can accept their interpretation as a good indication of its meaning partly because they had access to ancient traditions about what it meant, but mostly because neither Jesus nor Paul felt that it was necessary to correct any misconceptions they had on this point. The rabbis extended this "love" to include respect, because they allowed a woman to divorce a man who demanded that she do degrading things or refused to let her visit her relatives.[6] Peter may have had this concept of respect or honor in mind when he said, "Likewise, husbands, live with your wives in an understanding way, showing honor" (1 Pet 3:7).

What about couples who are no longer "in love" with each other—can they get divorced on the ground that there is a neglect of love? It would be very difficult to say that the modern concept of "being in love" can be read back into any text in the Bible, though it might be possible for someone to conclude that this was implied in the underlying principle of physical affection. However, Jesus' emphasis that divorce should occur only when there is "hardhearted" breaking of vows suggests that he would be against a divorce for something like "falling out of love," which does not involve the breaking of any vows or any actual harm to either partner.

Therefore, although the obligation of providing "conjugal love" in Exodus 21:10 can be regarded as the foundation of a principle of physical affection or even perhaps respect, it should not be spread so broadly that the concept of life-long marriage is weakened. Marriage is based on promises, not just on feelings. When the heat of passion cools, this is a signal not that the marriage is coming to an end but that the marriage needs attending to. No one sells their house just because the heating system needs repair!

SO WHAT CAN WE SAY TO THE ABUSED?

Now that we are aware that the grounds for divorce in the Bible include the principles of material support and physical affection, what do we say to the woman who has a violent, abusive husband? First, we can tell her that God's law has taken such sin into account. God's ideal for marriage is for a husband and wife to be faithful to each other and, as we saw in the Old Testament, for them to support each other with food, clothing and conjugal love. If these vows are broken, then there are grounds for divorce.

Since there is no question that the abusing husband is "neglecting" to support his wife, she should be aware that she does have the option to divorce him. Paul recognizes the validity of divorces when unbelievers have neglected their partners. And this also applies to Christians who break marriage vows: the fact that Paul did not expect Christians to act in this way does not mean they are not capable of it; Paul simply expected them to know better.

We should not forget, though, that Jesus emphasized forgiveness, as we saw in chapter five, so we should not advise this woman to divorce her husband the first time he breaks his vows. However, if he continues to sin hardheartedly (stubbornly or without repentance), Jesus says she may divorce him. In practice we have to depend on the individual concerned to decide when enough is enough, because we cannot know what goes on inside a marriage. We cannot know how much emotional abuse is happening, and even physical abuse is largely unseen or unreported.

BEHIND THE FAÇADE

We will never know how many of our friends return home to desperately sad and perhaps even dangerous situations. The façade of a "happy marriage" is often perpetuated by a whole family because they are ashamed to admit anything is wrong. A highly respected and successful man may go home each day to harangue or beat his wife and children, and a modest, quiet woman may meet a lover regularly or attack her husband with hurtful spite at every opportunity. But these are stereotypes, and no one who looks from the outside can guess what is really happening inside a front door.

One man told me, rather shamefacedly, about his former wife: outwardly she was a respectable and demure woman, but inside the home she always got her way and had a terrible temper. If she felt that her husband wasn't prompt enough in doing what she demanded, she would shout and strike him with whatever was at hand. He had been brought up not to hit women, so he would just try to defend himself while she continued striking him till her temper subsided or she got tired. On three occasions she broke his arm, which he had held up in defense. Once she managed to break his leg—I'm not sure how—and he never told the hospital staff what had actually happened.

He didn't divorce his wife, because he thought a Christian should not divorce on the grounds of abuse. During one hospital admission, however, a friend from a different church pointed out that one day she was likely to kill him and God couldn't possibly mean that to happen. He took this friend's advice, left her and eventually divorced her. When he did this, his church rejected him because they didn't know anything about the violence, and they regarded his wife as the victim of a completely groundless divorce. The story has a happy ending: he found a new wife, and they enjoy a wonderful life together. The Lord has certainly blessed his new marriage, and this husband and wife are both very active in another church.

Another true example of a false façade is a minister of a large church who frequently abused his wife. She was injured badly enough to need to go to the hospital on more than one occasion. His ministry was blessed by many conversions and a thriving congregation, but his happy family life was a sham. Few people know what his wife went through, but God knows.

Only the Lord really knows the heart; as Jesus said, evil comes from within and loves the dark. We cannot leave it up to a minister or a church leadership team to decide when a marriage ends; it is up to the individual victim, in prayer before the Lord. Only they and the Lord know what their life is really like. Only they know if their partner has expressed repentance, and only they will have to live with the consequences of the decision.

CONCLUSION: GOD KNOWS OUR SECRET SUFFERING

Our Lord knows the troubles we face in secret in our own home, things we never let others see because we are ashamed. People often feel that they have somehow caused their partner to be abusive or commit adultery, and sometimes there are indeed wrongs on both sides, but it does not excuse the offense. Often we can do things to heal the situation, but sometimes we cannot, and our Lord knows that too.

God has given us a very realistic law in the Old Testament, and he did not throw it away when Jesus came to transform us. We are not all transformed yet, and our world is still sinful until the kingdom of God fills the earth and everyone bends the knee to Jesus. Until then, we still need some of the God-given laws of the Old Testament: laws about murder, about injury, about marital neglect and abuse. The details do not always transfer well from one society to another, but Jesus highlights the principles and generalizes them for us (as we saw in detail in chapter four).

"God is not a ruler who sits on a high throne in isolation, ignorant of the suffering of his people. He aches with us, even in divorce, which he too has suffered. God loves you and knows your secret sufferings. He wants to help you and has given us practical laws to help deal with your hurt." *That* is what we say to a person in a neglectful or abusive marriage.

FURTHER READING

Divorce for Neglect Allowed by Shammaites and Other Jews

Instone-Brewer, David. *Divorce and Remarriage in the Bible.* Grand Rapids: Eerdmans, 2002. Chapter 5, "Rabbinic Teaching," summarizes the evidence from ancient Jewish sources.

Four Grounds for Divorce in Paul

Instone-Brewer, David. *Divorce and Remarriage in the Bible.* Grand Rapids: Eerdmans, 2002. Chapter 7, "Paul's Teaching," goes through the biblical text in much more detail.

9

CAN I GET MARRIED AGAIN?

A valid divorce implies the right to remarry.

We have seen that Jesus and Paul condemned easy groundless divorces, but what did they say about remarriage? This is a very difficult issue for Christians, mainly because the New Testament says so little. Jesus appears to condemn remarriage, though as we saw in chapter five, he was condemning it only after an invalid divorce. Paul is virtually silent on the issue, but there are two good reasons for believing that he allowed remarriage. First, we will see that everyone in the first century believed that divorcees could remarry—in fact, most people thought that they *should* remarry—and Paul says nothing to counter this belief. Second, we will see that while Paul does not say, "Divorcees can remarry," some of his teaching is based on the assumption that they can.

MARY AND JOSEPH'S DIVORCE CERTIFICATE

Did you know that we have found a divorce certificate of Mary and Joseph? It is dated A.D.72, so it was not *the* Mary and Joseph, who would have been about one hundred years old by that date. Mary was the most popular female name of the time, and Joseph was the second most popular male name, so it was likely that there were an awful lot of couples called Mary and Joseph. This particular couple were among a handful of Jews who were living on Masada during the final war against the Romans.

Masada was an impregnable fortress built by Herod the Great on top of a high rocky out-crop that was surrounded by steep sides. The only access was by a single very steep and easily defended path, so Herod made a safe and very comfortable haven for himself and a few privileged individuals. He had huge food stores and underground water cisterns the size of large basements. There were buildings for his servants and a beautifully decorated palace for himself. He even had a luxurious bathhouse with an under-floor heating system. When he died, the Romans left a small garri-son there but did not develop it in any way.

In A.D.66 the Romans invaded Palestine to put down a Jewish revolt. They besieged Jerusalem and eventually destroyed it in A.D.70, but some Jews had the foresight to capture Masada and fortify it against the Roman invasion. They managed to defend Masada till A.D.73, when the Romans finished the huge task of building an artificial slope against one of the sheer cliff sides of the fortress and then rolled their tall war engines up to the walls.

In the fortress the Romans found not just soldiers but whole families, who all killed themselves to avoid being captured—men, women and children. The Jews had converted the fortress into a small village and had filled the food stores, adapted one of the buildings into a synagogue with a school, and used a wall tower for a bakery. They had settled down and lived there in as normal a way as possible—within the constraints of being under siege by the Romans. People got married there, had children there and even got divorced there. We know this because some of them hid their most valuable documents and among these was the divorce certificate of Joseph and Mary, dated A.D.72.

"YOU ARE FREE TO MARRY ANY MAN YOU WISH"

This ancient document followed the traditional wording, including the only words that were compulsory in a Jewish divorce certificate: "You are free to marry any Jewish man you wish." Similar words are also found in many Greek certificates and convey the legal principle that the reason a divorce certificate was given to a woman was to enable her to remarry.

Everyone in the first century, so far as we know, agreed that a divorcee had the right to remarry. The Romans had this right enshrined in their law, and they certainly did not want to introduce any restriction to it. And as far as we know, there were no Jewish parties in the first century that prohibited remarriage after divorce.

WHAT THE DEAD SEA SCROLLS REALLY SAY

In the past some scholars thought that the writers of the Dead Sea Scrolls disapproved of remarriage, because one of the first of the scrolls to be discovered, the *Damascus Document,* appeared to say that you should not get married a second time.[1]

The scrolls of the community at Qumran were discovered in 1947 by an Arab boy looking for treasure. He was deliberately throwing stones into a cave high up in a cliff, and the sound of breaking pottery was exactly what he was hoping to hear. He did not climb up to it himself because he was afraid that the treasure might be protected by a *djinn* (genie) who had been released when he broke the pot. So he enlisted the help of his brother and a friend, by pretending that they were better climbers than he. He said that he would wait at the bottom, "ready to run for help" if there was a *djinn.* The boys were most disappointed when they found nothing more than crumbling documents, but they managed to sell a large scroll to an antique dealer in the market for a few dollars. This dealer recognized that it was a scroll of Isaiah, so he showed it to an Orthodox priest, who bought it for seventy dollars. Realizing that it was an ancient script, the priest sold it later for a million dollars—which shows the value of learning ancient Hebrew!

Among the scrolls, the text called the *Damascus Document* describes how a group of Jews deliberately chose to live in the desert to get away from a corrupt priesthood and from other Jews who they believed did not follow God's law properly. One of the things they criticized was the practice of having more than one wife at a time. Like Jesus, they said that God's plan for marriage was for it to be between one man and one woman. But early scholars misunderstood this passage and thought that the Qumran Jews were criticizing divorce and remarriage. We now know that this was wrong, because other scrolls show that this community allowed divorce. It has become clear that the *Damascus Document* was criticizing polygamy rather than remarriage—though some older books still repeat the early misunderstanding of this text. The Jews at Qumran, like all other Jews, regarded remarriage as the right of any divorcee.

EVERYONE EXPECTED DIVORCEES TO REMARRY

Actually both Jews and Romans in the first century thought that most divorcees *should* remarry. A Roman citizen who did not get remarried within eighteen months of a divorce (or within two years if their partner had died) could be prosecuted under a law that was enacted by Emperor Augustus in 18B.C. Augustus was concerned that many young men were avoiding marriage by divorcing the brides their parents had arranged for them to marry and then living carefree, licentious lives. He was also concerned that there were not enough children being born to Roman citizens, so he wanted these young men to get remarried and father children.

For their part, Jews thought that divorcees, especially childless ones, should remarry, because they had not yet obeyed the command "Be fruitful and multiply." They believed it was the duty of every Jewish man to father at least two children in order to fulfill this command, and if he had not done so before he was divorced or widowed, he was expected to remarry.

Remarriage for divorcees in the first century was therefore the norm; if they did not remarry, they were contravening the secular or religious law. And they all knew that they had the right to remarry because it was written into their divorce certificate: "You may marry any man you wish."

PAUL QUOTES A DIVORCE CERTIFICATE

These words, which were so well known from Jewish and Greco-Roman divorce certificates, are found in the New Testament, where Paul quotes a Christian version of them: "She is free to be married to whom she wishes, only in the Lord" (1 Cor 7:39).

When Jews wrote out their divorce certificates, they usually added the word *Jewish,* so that the words became "you may marry any *Jewish* man you wish." This reminded the ex-wife that she should remarry only within the faith. Paul makes a similar addition by telling Christian widows that they may remarry only "in the Lord"—that is, a Christian man. We do not know if Paul was converting the Jewish formula into a Christian one or whether he was quoting a traditional Christian version, but either way it would be very odd to quote these words if Christians disapproved altogether of remarriage after divorce.

It seems strange at first that Paul uses this phrase in verse 39, where he is speaking to widows and not to divorcées, but as we saw in chapter seven, it is because he wants to assure Christian widows that they do not need to follow the Jewish law of levirate marriage, which makes them marry their brother-in-law if they are childless. Paul argues that a widow has the same rights as a divorcee; if a divorcée can marry whomever she wishes, then a widow has this same right.

The interesting thing for us is that Paul's reasoning works only if you believe that divorcees *do* have the right to remarry. It would be no good assuring the widows that they had the same right as divorcées, to remarry anyone they wished, if divorcées were not in fact allowed to remarry. Paul was therefore assuming in this passage that his readers believed divorcees did have the right to remarry.

PAUL SAYS ABANDONED BELIEVERS CAN REMARRY

The only place where Paul specifically speaks about remarriage for a divorcee is when he addresses the believer who has been abandoned by their partner.

We saw in chapter six that separation was equivalent to divorce in Roman law, so that when someone was abandoned by their partner or was asked to leave their partner's house, they were being divorced. Paul was totally against this Roman groundless divorce-by-separation, just as Jesus was against the Jewish groundless divorce, and Paul told Christians who had separated from their partners that they should try to undo this divorce by attempting a reconciliation and remaining unmarried while they were doing so (1 Cor 7:11). But what if a believer was the victim of a Roman divorce-by-separation? We saw that Paul told them they were "not en- slaved" (1 Cor 7:15).

Some people interpret "not enslaved" as meaning "no longer tied to your partner" (that is, you can live apart but you cannot divorce), while others interpret it as "no longer tied to your marriage" (that is, you can get divorced but not remarry). Both these interpretations would have sounded like nonsense to a first- century reader because Paul was speaking to people who were *already divorced,* so they had no choice in the matter. It was no good telling them that they could live apart, because this was already forced on them, and it was no good telling them that they could get divorced, because as far as Roman law was concerned they were already divorced.

A first-century reader of Paul's letter would have had no doubt about what "not enslaved" meant, because it would remind them about the words on their divorce certificate: "You are now free to marry." Even if they did not have a divorce certificate (because many Roman divorces took place without an actual certifi- cate), they would still have had this right under

Roman law. Paul would have been understood to be saying very clearly, "You are no longer enslaved; you are free from that marriage and, as any divorce certificate says, free to remarry."

Paul granted this freedom to believers who were separated because their unbelieving partner had deserted them, but not to believers who had separated in such a way from their partner. He did not approve of groundless divorce, and if the believers had done the separating, he urged them to attempt reconciliation with their partners (1 Cor 7:11). However, when people were the victims of Roman divorce-by-separation they were powerless to reverse the situation, so Paul allowed them to regard their divorce as valid.

ABANDONMENT IS NEGLECT

What is Paul's justification for regarding this type of divorce as valid for the victim? On the face of it he is being inconsistent. He is saying on the one hand that divorce-by-separation is an invalid form of divorce, but on the other hand he allows the victim to remarry—which implies that he does think it is valid. There are two possible answers: he is being either legalistic or pragmatic.

Paul could be pointing out that the victims have been deserted and, as we have seen, under Jewish law they would then have a right to a divorce because they were suffering neglect as defined in Exodus 21:10-11—their partner was failing to provide food, clothing and conjugal love. It is likely that this was in Paul's mind, because speaking about being "enslaved" is a little strange in the context of marriage, but it is natural when speaking about Exodus 21:10, which originally concerned slavery.

Strictly speaking, although it is true that the victim had grounds for a biblical divorce (neglect), the divorce had not been properly processed according to Jewish custom. However, Paul may have been stating a practical solution that was fair to the victim even if it wasn't legally watertight. We have a very clear indication that Paul was thinking in this pragmatic way because he uses the phrase "God has called you to peace." This is similar to the rabbinic legal phrase "for the sake of peace," used by the courts when they gave a pragmatic solution in a case where a strict application of the law would be unfair. For example, strictly speaking, children could not be liable for theft, but leaving it at that would mean that children could take and keep anything they found. The rabbinic courts decided that this *was* stealing, though it would go without punishment. They could not justify this in strictly legal terms, so they made a ruling that was practical and fair. They said, "We do this for the sake of peace." Paul is saying the same thing, though he says this is God's ruling: "God has called you to peace."

Paul probably based his decision on both pragmatism *and* the application of the law of divorce for neglect. Either way, his decision makes good common sense that is fair to the victim, without approving of divorce-by-separation.

EVEN THE GUILTY PARTNER CAN REMARRY—EVENTUALLY

Paul allows the victims of a groundless divorce to get remarried, but what about the people who carried out these divorces—can they ever get remarried? On the face of it the answer is "No," or at least "Not for some time." This is because Paul gives very clear instructions in 1 Corinthians 7:11 that the people who have separated from their partners must remain unmarried and attempt to be reconciled with the people whom they have divorced.

Paul does not say how long someone should continue to remain unmarried and attempt reconciliation, and many interpreters assume that this person may never remarry. However, Paul's instruction is not a punishment but an attempt to help the victim of that divorce. He is telling the people who forced their partners into an unwarranted divorce that they should try to put things right by giving their ex-partners the opportunity to continue the marriage—or, strictly speaking, to remarry them. This implies that when it is *no longer possible* to reverse the mistake, the command is no longer in force, because it can no longer be carried out. If the divorced partner marries someone else or rejects all the attempts at reconciliation, then we can assume that the person can stop trying for reconciliation and can remarry.

It would certainly be strange if the command not to remarry were a punishment for groundless divorce, for this would make it into an unforgivable sin, and we know that there is only one of these (Mt 12:31). One might argue that the inability to remarry is a *consequence* but not a punishment, because the former marriage is still carrying on in some spiritual way or in God's eyes. This reasoning works only if *no one* can remarry after a divorce, because if the wronged partner can remarry (as I have concluded in this book) then the marriage is over. We saw in chapter seven that the concept that only death can end a marriage is not scriptural and is based on a misunderstanding of a few texts.

Therefore the command that "guilty" partners should avoid remarriage is not a consequence nor a punishment but a practical way for them to try to reverse their mistake, and the command lasts only as long as this might still be possible. In practice, few people who divorce others against their will would bother to obey this command unless, like these Corinthians, they were convicted that they had done something wrong soon after the divorce. But what if they were convicted of the error long after they had divorced, when one or both of the former spouses had already remarried? Should they attempt to divorce their new partners in order to be reconciled and remarry their original partners? We will look at this in the next chapter.

CONCLUSION: PAUL ALLOWS REMARRIAGE

I am sure that if Paul had told Christians that they should never remarry they would have obeyed, even though it would have meant breaking the Roman law and putting them in danger of prosecution, and even if they did not yet have any children so that they were also breaking the Jewish laws of piety. Just as some of them were willing to face lions and torturers because they refused to say "Caesar is Lord," I am sure that they would have been willing to break the laws that commanded remarriage—*if* Paul had told them to.

We have seen in previous chapters that Jesus and Paul told only those who had invalid divorces to avoid remarriage, which implies that those who had valid divorces were allowed to remarry. In this chapter we found that Paul's teaching *assumes* that divorcees can remarry, but we are still left with the fact that Jesus and Paul did not *specifically* say that divorcees may remarry. Can we safely assume that they can, simply based on this silence?

Silence on this issue is not strange. Actually it would be strange if Paul made a pronouncement that divorcees were allowed to remarry, because the question never arose in the first century. It would be like saying "Married women may have children" or "A married couple may sleep in the same bed"—there was no need to say them because these things inhered in the nature and purpose of marriage. There was even less reason to say "A divorcee may remarry," because not only was the right of remarriage regarded as part of the very nature of divorce, but divorcees had a legal certificate that said precisely this. If we said that Paul's silence means that he condemned remarriage, then we would also have to assume that his silence condemned breastfeeding by Christians or celebrating birthdays or adopting children or any number of things that were considered normal activities by everyone in the ancient world.

We therefore have to conclude that Paul allowed validly divorced believers to remarry. If they had *initiated* the invalid Roman divorce-by-separation, he tells them they should not remarry but try to reverse the divorce instead. But if they were *victims* of this kind of divorce, they could not do anything to reverse it, so they could regard it as a valid divorce based on neglect. Paul even quoted the words of the divorce certificate with approval, and his words "not enslaved" would be unambiguous to a first-century reader.

His teaching on remarriage is admittedly ambiguous to modern readers, and we will look in chapter twelve at the reasons why our perception has changed so dramatically. Before that, however, we have to look at the difficult situation of those who *have* divorced but cannot say that their divorce was based on biblical grounds.

FURTHER READING

Early Jewish Divorce Certificates

Instone-Brewer, David. "1 Corinthians 7 in the Light of the Jewish, Greek and Aramaic Marriage and Divorce Papyri." *Tyndale Bulletin* 52 (2001):225-43. Analyzes some typical documents from the first two centuries.

_____. *Divorce and Remarriage in the Bible.* Grand Rapids: Eerdmans, 2002. Chapter 5, "Rabbinic Teaching," examines especially the Masada divorce certificate in the light of rabbinic teaching.

Discoveries at Masada

Archer, J. Leone. *Her Price Is Beyond Rubies: The Jewish Woman in Greco-Roman Palestine.* Sheffield, U.K.: Sheffield Academic Press, 1990. Archer was the first to provide English translations of all the important divorce and marriage certificates from Masada and the

Judean desert, as well as discussing the whole subject.

Yadin, Yigael. *Masada: Herod's Fortress and the Zealots' Last Stand.* London: Cardinal, 1973. Yadin did much of the original excavation, and his book is a colorful and readable account of the history of the site.

Paul's Allowing Remarriage

Instone-Brewer, David. *Divorce and Remarriage in the Bible.* Grand Rapids: Eerdmans, 2002. Chapter 7, "Paul's Teaching," looks at the texts from Paul's writings in more detail than I do here.

Keener, Craig.... *And Marries Another: Divorce and Remarriage in the Teaching of the New Testament.* Peabody, Mass.: Hendrickson, 1991. Very good at presenting Paul's teaching in light of the Greco-Roman world.

10

IS REMARRIAGE ADULTERY?

Don't redivorce, because two wrongs don't make a right.

We have considered Jesus and Paul's teaching about remarriage after a biblically valid divorce, but we are now faced with another question. Do people whose divorces were *not* biblically valid have to stay unmarried for the rest of their life? Didn't Jesus say that remarriage after an invalid divorce is committing adultery? And what if you have already gotten married after an invalid divorce? Are you supposed to get divorced from this new marriage because remarriage is not allowed?

JOSEPH'S PLAN TO DIVORCE MARY

Nativity plays are invitations to disaster. You are probably familiar with the story of how a little boy playing the innkeeper got his revenge for not being given the part of Joseph. He opened the door with a triumphant smile: "Of course, there's room—come on in!"

Or how about the Joseph who disgustedly looked inside the inn door and replied, "I wouldn't let Mary stay in this dump any-way—we'll be much better off in the stable."

A church in north London decided to add authen-ticity by using a real oil lamp and real straw. Predictably, a child knocked over the lamp, which set fire to the straw, and the authenticity of the scene had to be sacrificed with the use of a modern fire extinguisher. As a local news-paper reported, "No children were hurt but baby Jesus melted."

The real Christmas story involved many more potential disasters. The wise men might have returned to Herod, or his soldiers could have arrived before Jesus' family left Bethlehem. God had to employ his angels as stage prompters in order to avoid these disasters. The first po-tential calamity to be averted by an angel was Joseph's intention to divorce his betrothed wife, Mary, for her seeming infidelity. Joseph consid-ered using an "Any Cause" divorce for the best of reasons—he wanted to avoid subjecting Mary to the shame of a public court (Mt 1:19). But as we saw in chapter five, Jesus taught that the "Any Cause" divorce was invalid. So the first nativity story almost started and ended with an invalid divorce!

AN INVALID DIVORCE FOR VALID REASONS

Joseph was planning to use the "Any Cause" divorce in order to save Mary from shame, but would this have meant that he had an invalid divorce? In our modern day there are many similar situations, where a divorce is granted without the citation of any specific fault because the adulterous partner has agreed not to contest the divorce. Similarly, someone who is suffering abuse may separate from their partner and later get a divorce based on that separation, without actually saying anything about the abuse in the divorce petition. Must we conclude that the wronged partner has a biblically invalid divorce in these situations because they were not divorced on valid biblical grounds?

We saw a similar situation in the previous chapter where Paul recognized a divorce as valid even though no biblical grounds were cited to enact it. This was the case of someone who was the victim of a divorce-by-separation. Paul looks behind the divorce to see what actually caused it—the biblical grounds of neglect when they were abandoned—and recognizes that even if the divorce procedure did not actually name the biblical ground, it was nonetheless the reason for the divorce. He therefore tells the wronged partner that they are "not enslaved" (1 Cor 7:15), that is, they could divorce and remarry.

INVALID DIVORCE FOR NO GOOD REASON

If a divorce was invalid and one of them had remarried, should they then divorce their second partner and return to their first in order to put things right? Many people think that they should do so, and some have even done it, but since this results in yet another marriage breakup (of the second marriage) it is difficult to justify.

If anyone did act on this teaching and divorce their new husband or wife, it would be like trying to put right a wrong by committing another wrong. Two wrongs don't make a right, as they say, and the injury caused by breaking one set of marriage vows cannot be healed by doing the same wrong to someone else.

184

Imagine a person who hears an ecologist say, "If you have hardwood kitchen cabinets, you are helping to destroy valuable rain forests," and goes home, tears out his expensive mahogany kitchen cupboards and replaces them with pine ones. This drastic action does not help anyone and merely results in utterly wasting the valuable mahogany. The ecologist communicated her message in a dramatic way to get attention and to bring home the importance and relevance of the subject, but she did not expect anyone to tear out their kitchen cabinetry, because this would not help the situation and would only compound the mistake.

Jesus makes a similarly dramatic statement when he says, "If you have remarried after an invalid divorce, you are committing adultery." He is pointing out the serious implications of an invalid divorce in the most forceful way possible. He says, in effect, "No one should ignore the invalidity of 'Any Cause' divorces, for technically anyone who remarries after one is committing adultery." The Gospel writers do not record the word *technically,* however, and I do not think that Jesus would have used a word like this because it would dilute the shock of the message. It has far more impact to say, "If you remarry, you are an adulterer."

PREACHERS' RHETORIC

Preachers often make similar statements. They say things like "If you do not share the gospel with your neighbor, you are opening the door to hell for them," or "Looking at pornography is committing adultery against your wife." This second example is based on what Jesus said in Matthew 5:28: "Everyone who looks at a woman with lustful intent has already committed adultery with her in his heart." Another bold declaration made by Jesus is "Everyone who is angry with his brother will be liable to judgment" for murder (Mt 5:22). He did not mean, however, that this person should be punished as if they had committed murder, and neither did he mean that a person should be punished for adultery if they had looked at someone lustfully or if they had remarried after a technically invalid divorce.

Some people in the early church did take this kind of preaching by Jesus literally, including the teaching "If your right eye causes you to sin, tear it out" (Mt 5:29). In the early second century a man called Democritus did this, and Tertullian had to warn other Christians not to copy his example (*Apology* 46.11-12). Another second-century church father, Origen, actually castrated himself in order to fulfill the command

"If your right hand causes you to sin, cut it off and throw it away. For it is better that you lose one of your members than that your whole body go into hell." Paradoxically, later in life he interpreted this same text with a nonliteral rhetorical meaning.

It seems self-evident that Jesus was using preacher's rhetoric here and did not expect us to act on it literally. If we did literally follow all of Jesus' rhetorical teachings, we would have to put the man who loses his temper in prison and tell the wife of someone who looks lustfully at another woman that she has grounds for divorce, and a large proportion of Christians would be self-maimed.

Matthew gathered these examples of preaching rhetoric into a single passage, Matthew 5:21-32, ending with the teaching that remarriage after invalid divorce is adultery. It followed immediately after Jesus' statement that lust is adultery and that we should "cut off" the body part that leads to lust. By putting Jesus' saying about remarriage in this context, Matthew was clearly implying that Jesus was not speaking in a literal way. He did not expect anyone to act as though remarriage is literally adultery any more than he expected them to act as though lust is literally adultery.

NO ONE SAYS GET DIVORCED AGAIN

The specific words that Jesus used make it clearer still that he did not expect us to carry out a divorce. Although about the roving eye he said, "Tear it out," and about the erring hand he said, "Cut it off," he did not say to the remarried, "Get divorced." If we do not literally act on the commands Jesus did state ("tear it out" and "cut it off"), it would certainly be wrong for us to presume to act on a command that Jesus did *not* state ("get divorced").

Paul must also have come across this problem on many occasions, because a large number of Christian converts would have been divorcees. Roman citizens walked in and out of marriages frequently, and virtually all of their divorces would have been without valid grounds. Paul did not say anything in any of his letters to people in this situation, which presumably means that he did not think they needed to do anything. As we saw in chapter nine, he took a very practical approach to the situation of believers who had been abandoned by their partners, telling them that they were "not enslaved" because "God has called you to peace," and he probably applied the same pragmatism to this situation. In other words, he treated their invalid divorces as if they were actually valid, on the pragmatic grounds that the divorced-and-remarried person could not now put things right.

Therefore, although Jesus pointed out that virtually all Jewish remarriages were technically adulterous, neither he nor Paul told these remarried couples to get divorced or to try to rectify the situation in any other way.

INVALID DIVORCES BEFORE CONVERSION

Some churches say that a new Christian starts their life from scratch, so that an invalid divorce that they had before they became a Christian does not count. This is based on the assumption that any vows that they made before they became Christians were not taken before God so they do not carry the same force.

This view implies that God disregards the vows of non-Christians and that the marriages of non-Christians are somehow less valid. It also implies that a new Christian's present marriage may be substandard because they made their vows while they were still non-Christians. Although most churches that have this type of policy would nonetheless affirm the validity of marriage vows by non-Christians, their stand-point still assumes that vows made before a person became a Christian can be broken, whereas vows by Christians cannot.

This is similar to the way in which some of the people in Corinth were thinking, and Paul was keen to correct them. When they became Christians they started to regard their former life with contempt, and for some of them this included their marriage partner. They thought that they should divorce their nonbelieving partner in order to be better Christians, but Paul tells them they are not allowed to do this (1 Cor 7:12-14). He says that if their unbelieving partner is willing to stay married, the Christian partner should certainly not be the one who breaks up the marriage, because God recognizes a marriage between nonbelievers just as much as a marriage between two believers.

Paul tells Christians to remain with their non-Christian partners if it is at all possible, and he does not regard a marriage that was contracted before they became Christians as any less permanent than one that is contracted after. He does say that if unbelieving partners want to leave then believers should let them do so. This does not imply that breaking up marriages to nonbelievers is less terrible than breaking up marriages between believers, but simply that they have to let unbelievers leave because there isn't anything they can do to stop them.

When we become Christians we are new creations, and we start from scratch without any sin, but we do not start from scratch with regard to our marriages and other commitments such as loans and business contracts. We should be even *more* committed to keeping promises and vows that we made when we were not Christians.

DECIDING INNOCENCE OR GUILT

Although we have found that remarriage is possible even after an invalid divorce, this does not minimize the sin of breaking up the previous marriage. Like any sin, it can be repented of and forgiven. Yet some churches consider this sin so serious that they will refuse to remarry the guilty partner after a divorce, or either partner after a groundless divorce.

I do not agree with this position: as I said at the end of the previous chapter, I think that a church should remarry someone even if that person had forced a wronged partner into a divorce—though only after that person has gone back to their former partner with a genuine offer of reconciliation and has truly repented of this sin. But I can appreciate that some churches will not want to remarry such people on these premises, and this is, of course, a perfectly valid decision for them to make. However, churches that have policies based on innocence or guilt in a divorce need some kind of procedure for deciding what actually caused the breakup of the marriage.

It is very difficult to decide guilt and innocence without a court trial, because without the formalities of evidence and cross-examination it is usually the loudest people who get their viewpoints heard and the other partners are often unable to present their sides of the stories. But even if divorces go to trial, a secular court does not decide guilt on the biblical basis of breaking marriage vows, and so the church is still left without any authoritative decision.

In some churches the elders or bishop may wish to investigate the divorce. As I suggested at the end of chapter eight, though, it is very difficult for others to really know what takes place in private behind the façade of a normal marriage. I have come across too many instances where a wronged partner is ostracized by a church—the wife of a highly respected minister who in private has been abusive or unfaithful, or a husband who is assumed to be guilty of some unknown sin because his wife has walked out on him. Only God can reliably judge who is the guilty and who is the wronged partner. In any case, by the time most marriages break up, both partners have broken their vows to support each other.

My own practice therefore is not to attempt to judge who is innocent and who is guilty. I feel that it is better to leave justice and forgiveness to God. This does not mean that we should ignore the sin of breaking up a marriage, but we should remember that we are not the ones against whom the sin has been committed. The people who break their marriage vows have sinned against their partners and against God before whom those vows were made, and they should ask forgiveness from both of them. I therefore always have a service of repentance for broken promises before any marriage involving a divorcee—as explained in the next chapter.

CONCLUSION: DIVORCE IS FORGIVABLE

We have seen that the sin of marriage breakup is very serious, but God forgives a repentant divorcee just as he forgives all other sinners. That does not mean that there will not be consequences to suffer as a result of this sin—all divorces cause suffering, and the suffering from a marriage breakup can last a lifetime—but it does mean that the consequences of the sin can stop getting worse. Therefore, a remarried divorcee *should not* divorce his or her new partner, because this would be the cause of even more suffering. Interpreting Jesus' words in this way would be as erroneous as concluding that we should literally cut off parts of our bodies that cause us to sin.

Our God is a loving Father who knows the failings of his children. He knows the foolish and self-destructive things we do, and he helps us to prevent them and brings healing afterward. He offers us wisdom in his Word, warning us not to break marriage vows; then he tells us to reverse our foolishness if it is still possible. And even when it is no longer possible to put right the wrong we have done, he still offers us forgiveness and leads us forward.

11

PROMISES, PROMISES

Marriage vows and remarriage in church.

When you sign a contract, do you read the small print? We know we should, but it's such a chore that we usually don't bother. What about when you got married? Did you read the small print then? Perhaps you did not realize there was any, because the small print in a marriage service consists of the marriage vows. You promised to love, honor and keep, and perhaps to obey. The wording varies, but it has remained remarkably similar for centuries, and we can trace the vows right back to the Old Testament.

THE EARLIEST ENGLISH MARRIAGE SERVICE

One vow has changed: in the earliest English marriage services the bride's vows included a promise to "be bonny and buxom in bed and at board." This wonderfully alliterative phrase comes from the Use of Sarum, the earliest English marriage service I have found, which was authorized by the bishop of Salisbury in 1085.

In this very early version some of the vows are still in Latin, while others are in Old English. The whole service is almost identical to our modern version, except that now the Latin has been translated and the line about the bonny and buxom bride has been omitted.

Originally these words meant something rather different from now. *Bonny* is from the French *bon,* or "good"; *buxom* is from an old German word meaning "pliant" or "obedient"; *board* is where you put food (the sideboard), so this means mealtimes; and *bed* simply meant "nighttime." So "be bonny and buxom in bed and at board" meant "behave properly and obediently through night and day." The meanings of these words changed over the years, and the church objected to talking about bonny and buxom brides in bed, so we have now lost this vow.

The other marriage vows have survived intact, and this is very fortunate, because they come from the New Testament. Both bride and groom make promises to each other that they will "love, honor and keep" or "love, nourish and cherish," or something equivalent. The exact words vary, but these basic ideas are always present because they come from Ephesians: "Husbands should love their wives as their own bodies. He who loves his wife loves himself. For no one ever hated his own flesh, but nourishes and cherishes it, just as Christ does the church" (Eph 5:28-29).

OUR MARRIAGE VOWS COME FROM EXODUS 21

Paul said that husbands should love, nourish and cherish their brides as Christ loves, nourishes and cherishes the church. He was saying that Christ keeps the same marriage vows with regard to the church that a groom makes to his bride. The words translated "nourishes and cherishes" mean "to feed" and "to keep warm." They are intimate words usually applied to feeding and caring for children or other loved ones, and Paul is therefore saying that every groom should love, feed and clothe his wife—exactly the same three obligations that we found in Exodus 21:10.

These same vows are expressed in a wider variety of language in Jewish marriage contracts. As well as intimate terms like *nourish* and *cherish,* they use more general terms like "care for" and "honor" instead of "feed and clothe." Christian marriages also employ a wide variety of language, perhaps partly through the influence of the synagogue, which also influenced the language of Ephesians. All these variations in Christian and Jewish marriage vows can be traced back to the wording of Exodus 21:10.

The Christian wedding service preserved these vows more accurately than Jewish marriage contracts, especially the vow of "conjugal love"—for example, when it included the beautiful phrase "with my body I worship you."

All three vows were articulated in first- and second-century Jewish marriage certificates, where bride and groom promised each other "food, clothing and bed," but later Jewish marriage certificates omit even this euphemistic reference to conjugal activity. However, Jewish marriage contracts are very useful for tracing the gradual change from a straightforward quotation of Exodus 21:10, "food and clothing and conjugal love," to more general terms like "care for" and "honor."

VALUABLE CONTRACTS IN THE RUBBISH ROOM

The best collection of early Jewish marriage contracts comes from a huge collection of documents that were rescued from a rubbish room in the Cairo synagogue by two women in the 1890s. Agnes Smith Lewis and Margaret Dunlop Gibson were twin sisters who became two of the most remarkable female scholars in biblical studies. When they had both been widowed, they set off on a tour of the Middle East, where their ability to read ancient texts in Hebrew, Greek, Syriac and Arabic made them welcome even in male-only establishments like the library of the Sinai Monastery. There they recognized and rescued a vellum page from a valuable fifth-century Gospel in Old Syriac, which was being used as a butter dish. Another great discovery was original Hebrew manuscripts of Ecclesiasticus, which till then was known only in its Greek translation. It was this discovery that led them to the Cairo synagogue and its sacred rubbish room, or *geniza.*

A *geniza* was where Jews deposited documents and books that were no longer wanted but that could not be thrown away because they contained the written name of God. These included any Scripture text that had become worn or damaged; it had to be thrown away so that no one would make mistakes while reading it. Jews threw private contracts, such as wills and documents of marriage or divorce, into a *geniza* because these, too, contained the name of God. Every few years they emptied the *geniza* by putting all the documents and books in a coffin and burying them with a full Jewish funeral service.

The *geniza* at Cairo was special because it had been neglected and had not been emptied for about a thousand years! With the help of Solomon Schechter, the women got the permission of the synagogue authorities to take the most valuable of these documents for scholars to study in Cambridge. They filled several tea chests with so many documents that Cambridge University Library has only recently finished the huge job of cataloging and preserving them all, and many are still awaiting detailed study.

Recent studies of the marriage contracts in this *geniza* collection have clearly shown that the origin of the words "honor," "care for," "keep" and "cherish" in marriage vows can be traced back to the vows to feed and clothe in Exodus 21.

THE VOW "TO OBEY"

The vow to obey, which for a time was used in most Jewish and Christian marriages, is very different from the other marriage vows: it is not found in Exodus 21; it is not referred to anywhere else in the Old Testament as a marriage vow; and it is one-sided, because usually only the woman promises it.

Did you or your partner promise to obey when you got married? Perhaps you were not listening during that part of the marriage service and you can't remember what promises you made to each other! Some services still include "obey" and others omit it. When I conduct a marriage service, I always give couples the choice to include it or not and ask them to decide together long before the wedding which vows each of them will make. Their consideration of this issue sometimes produces heated debates and even arguments! But it is better to argue about this and other presuppositions *before* you get married than wake up on your first morning at home and argue about who is making the breakfast!

If you do not have any problems with the vow to obey you can skip the next couple of sections. Some people insist on this vow, while others regard it as un-Christian. If you have already made up your mind, I cannot go into enough detail here to change your viewpoint, though you might be interested to know the historic reasons for including this vow.

ROMAN WOMEN REBELLED AGAINST SUBMISSION

The vow of obedience originates in Greek moral regulations and not in the Old Testament law, for although women submitted in practice to their husbands in most Old Testament cultures, such submission became a *moral rule* only in Greek culture. This rule was also important in Roman times, and it gained huge importance during the first century A.D. (during the time of the New Testament), because issues of women's rights were starting to get out of hand.

Roman women began to seek more and more rights and to demand all the same freedoms that men had, including the freedom to be sexually immoral. They took lovers like their husbands, got drunk like their husbands and squandered money like their husbands. While their husbands wasted money on chariot racing and on buildings that aggrandized their reputations, their wives spent huge sums on jewelry and hairstyling. The longing for freedom also started to spread to children and slaves, so that children demanded to have whatever they wanted and slaves went on strike. Soon the whole of "decent" society felt threatened by this drive for freedom.

Moral philosophers tried to stop the rot by harking back to the good old days, as had been epitomized in the writings of Aristotle (384-322B.C.). He was the great philosopher who taught that society is built on the foundation of the family, with the man as the head of the household. The wife should submit to him as her husband, the children should submit to him as their father, and the household slaves should submit to him as their master. When everyone submitted to the head of the house, conflict would disappear, and the whole of society would be harmonious. The Romans regarded this philosophy as a way of coping with the moral breakdown of their society. Women who obeyed did not get drunk or take lovers; children who obeyed were diligent to listen to the slaves who tutored them; and slaves who obeyed did not steal or go on strike.

Most respectable women were appalled by the excesses of the "freedom" movement, so they were careful to show their submissiveness to their husband, in public at least. A woman who exercised her freedom by not being submissive was assumed to be free in her morality too. This was a prejudice, of course; similarly nowadays, many people assume that a woman who goes into a bar by herself has an immoral lifestyle, so to avoid this assumption, many women avoid bars. The only way for a woman to evade suspicions of immorality in the first century was to be submissive to her husband or father, and the only generally accepted concept of a moral household was a submissive one.

Moral tracts from all branches of society, including Judaism and the Isis religion, urged their adherents to follow this threefold code of submission by wives, children and slaves in order to demonstrate that they were living a moral lifestyle. The New Testament also teaches this threefold submission, though its authors betray some discomfort with the society's moral code by adding caveats to it. In Ephesians, for example, we have the familiar Aristotelian list of submission—wives to husbands, children to fathers, and slaves to masters—but each of these has a Christian comment added to it:

- Wives should submit, *but* husbands should love their wives sacrificially (Eph 5:22-33).

- Children should submit, *but* fathers should not provoke them (Eph 6:1-4).

- Slaves should submit, *but* masters should not threaten them (Eph 6:5-9).

The moral code of submission appears in several other places in the New Testament as well, but always with Christian comments added: see Colossians 3:18-4:11; 1 Timothy 2:9-15; 6:1-2; and 1 Peter 2:18-3:7.

WHY EARLY CHRISTIANS DECIDED TO SUBMIT

The New Testament writers clearly have severe misgivings about this Aristotelian moral code, but Christians were nevertheless taught to keep it. This was simply because the code defined morality in general society, and if Christians ignored it they would give the impression that they were immoral. They therefore decided to follow the code but with some Christian limitations.

Paul explains his motives for teaching Greek morality to Titus and Timothy, whom he was training as church leaders. He tells Titus that he must teach women to be "submissive to their own husbands, that the word of God may not be reviled" (Tit 2:5)—that is, so that outsiders would not think that Christians are immoral. He says that slaves must submit to their masters for a similar reason: "Teach slaves to be subject to their masters in everything ... so that in every way they will make the teaching about God our Savior attractive" (Tit 2:9-10 NIV).[1] And he says the same thing to Timothy: "Let all who are under a yoke as slaves regard their own masters as worthy of all honor, so that the name of God and the teaching may not be reviled" (1 Tim 6:1).

Peter had similar motives, as he explains when he says that wives should submit to their husbands especially if their husbands are not Christians, because these men would be won over by their wives' moral behavior (1 Pet 3:1-2). Peter also adds that they should avoid other appearances of freedom that first-century women were exploiting, such as squandering money on "braiding of hair, the wearing of gold, or the putting on of fine clothing" (1 Pet 3:3).

Christian women, children and slaves in the first century were willing to follow the Aristotelian model of morality in order to avoid slandering the gospel. Many Christians today continue to follow this moral code, though usually for different reasons. Some today, like the Amish, avoid jewelry and fine clothes, and others teach submission to husbands and fathers, though of course no one still teaches submission of slaves. Most modern Christians who follow this lifestyle do so because they regard it as a God-given guide for a harmonious family life. Very few people do it for the same reason as the early Christians—that is, in order to aid evangelism.

SHOULD BOTH BRIDE AND GROOM PROMISE TO "OBEY"?

We cannot come to a definite conclusion here, but it is an important subject for couples to think about together, especially if one or both of you have made this vow or are thinking of making it.

If one or both partners feel that a vow of obedience should be made, I would suggest that the groom as well as the bride should make it. Paul probably has this in mind when he prefaces his words to husbands, wives, children and slaves with the injunction that they should "submit to one another" (Eph 5:21). This was completely opposite to the Aristotelian model, where everyone submitted to the father of the house in order to give a clear line of command. Paul says that submission can be a two-way relationship. He emphasizes this when he says that a husband should love his wife sacrificially (Eph 5:25), that a father should teach his children (a job normally left to slaves—Eph 6:4) and that a master should remember that he and his slaves share the same Master in heaven (Eph 6:9).

In most of the Jewish marriage contracts found in the Cairo *geniza,* either the bride or groom do not make a vow of obedience at all or it is just made by the bride. But in a few contracts both the bride and groom promise to submit to each other, as Paul suggests. We do not know whether Paul was the first to suggest this, but it is unlikely that Jews would have followed his teaching, so perhaps some Jews already practiced mutual submission in the first century. Whatever the origin, it is a good model to follow, because it has a solid basis in the New Testament while including the concepts of both submission and equality. Whatever you decide to include in marriage vows, it should be a joint decision between bride and groom, because if you disagree on this, the marriage will not last long.

These vows are among the most serious promises we ever make. They are made before God and in the hearing of the most important people in our lives. Our relatives and friends are there not just as witnesses but as potential supporters who may help us if our marriage ever starts to go wrong or if we fall into situations where we are tempted to break our vows. A life-long commitment to another person is difficult and daunting, and we need all the help that others can give us.

Tragically, these vows are sometimes broken, and the damage is sometimes so severe that the wronged partner reluctantly decides that the marriage is over. Even more tragically, some marriages are legally dissolved even without broken vows, or the decision to divorce is taken by the guilty partner against the wishes of the wronged one. Should we allow a divorcee to repeat the same vows in church to another person?

WHEN SHOULD WE REFUSE REMARRIAGE IN CHURCH?

The traditional reason for forbidding remarriage in church is the belief that a marriage continues in some mystical way until a former partner dies. In chapter seven we found that this traditional church teaching is based on a misunderstanding of a few texts that first-century believers would have understood very differently. However, it is understandable that, for some churches, the history of almost unanimous traditional interpretations may outweigh this insight into how first-century believers understood these same texts.

A church could decide to refuse remarriage to anyone who was the guilty partner in a divorce, but I don't think this is a practical option because it is often impossible to decide who was guilty and who was innocent. In most cases it is like trying to work out which of two children started a fight. I argued in chapter ten that Paul probably allowed the guilty partner to remarry if an attempt at reconciliation failed—though this is very uncertain.

There is one situation in which a church perhaps *should* refuse to conduct a wedding, and that is when a divorcee wants to marry the lover with whom they committed adultery. Conducting a wedding in this situation would be like condoning the sin that broke up the former marriage. The early rabbis actually made an absolute rule to prohibit this, which was very wise and practical because it helped to discourage adultery. It ensured that if your marriage was falling apart and you fell in love with someone else, the *last* thing you would do was commit adultery, because it would mean that you could never get married to your lover even if your marriage did end in divorce. Although I cannot find biblical support for this rule, I believe it is certainly worth considering, though unfortunately it won't really be effective unless it becomes generally accepted in all Christian churches.

HELPING DIVORCEES KNOW GOD'S FORGIVENESS

The strongest reason for allowing remarriage in church is that if we refuse it we are saying, on God's behalf, that he does not want that couple to remarry. God forgives sin, and if we really believe this we must also believe that sinners are allowed to move on after repentance. We need to demonstrate that breaking marriage vows is a terrible sin, while at the same time teaching that God is able and willing to forgive this sin.

There is rarely any need to emphasize the sinfulness of marriage breakup to someone remarrying in church, because if you ever find yourself as a bride or groom at the front of a church for the second time, I can guarantee that you will feel guilty. When you had already previously promised to keep your vows "till death us do part," it seems hypocritical to promise the same thing to another person. Even if it was not your fault that the marriage broke down, you may still feel the congregation and even God himself judging you. You know that God understands and that he forgives the repentant sinner, but knowing this doesn't stop you from feeling hypocritical.

I have lived through these feelings with many couples, and often someone who was clearly an innocent victim of a divorce feels just as much guilt as a person who caused a breakup. They took their vows seriously the first time and are just as serious this time. They want reassurance that their sins are forgiven, and they want God to help them do better this time.

SERVICE OF REPENTANCE FOR BROKEN VOWS

I have found it very useful to have an informal service of repentance for broken promises shortly before the wedding. In fact I insist on this for all weddings that involve a partner who has been divorced, because I have found that those who are most aware of their previous broken vows *want* this service and those who are not sufficiently aware of their guilt *need* it.

I invite both partners to take part in the service of repentance, whether or not they are both divorced, and all three of us ask for God's for- giveness for broken promises because we are all guilty of this at some time. This does not diminish the uniqueness of marriage vows or the seriousness of breaking them, but it does emphasize that all sins are serious and all sins are forgivable. The service consists of a short prayer time, perhaps with a reading. You may find the following prayer useful, or you may prepare something similar. It is useful to have the prayer written down so that all three can pray it aloud together.

> Heavenly Father, who has cared for me from my birth and who has promised to love me unconditionally, I come to you in repentance. I confess that I have made promises to you and to others that I have not kept. I have promised to pray for people or promised to love and care for them, and I have not kept these promises as I should. Please forgive me for my sin and give comfort to those whom I have let down and hurt. Give me strength for the future to be able to keep the promises that I will make. I ask you these things in the name of our Lord Jesus. Amen.

The minister can follow with a prayer for the couple's future life together.

The best time and place for this is just after the wedding rehearsal, which is usually the day before the wedding in the place where the couple will marry. The rehearsal will probably have made them think about their vows already, so it is an ideal time to ask God to forgive their past and help them with the future. Most Christian divorcees will already have asked God's forgiveness for any part they played in their marriage breakups, so an important aspect of this service is an affirmation of forgiveness.

Couples have told me that this simple service gave them a real sense of God's forgiveness, and that they were able to face their wedding with a clear conscience and a sense of God's strength to make a success of their new marriage. Although I insist on this service for any marriage involving a divorcees, I have never had to force the issue—everyone has been willing to take part. In fact most of them are very happy to do so and some said that they were relieved that someone had finally taken their former promises seriously.

CONCLUSION: MARRIAGE VOWS ARE THE KEY

Marriage vows are central to the wedding service and the foundation of a life together. Allowing remarriage in church does not diminish the importance of vows, so long as we make sure that there is sufficient recognition that breaking marriage vows is sinful and requires repentance and forgiveness.

The biblical vows have survived intact from their origins in the book of Exodus, via the Jewish marriage contracts and the letter to the Ephesians, and through to the early English marriage services, where they have remained almost unchanged for the last thousand years. The language has evolved from "love, clothe and feed" to more general terms like "love, honor and cherish," but the underlying principles have remained the same—material support and physical affection. When we marry, we make these promises to each other, and when we break them, the marriage starts to break down, because when we fail to love and honor and cherish each other, what is left?

The Holy Spirit has ensured that we still make the same marriage vows that God recommended through Moses, even though the church has forgotten their origin. It is remarkable that these vows have been preserved when we consider that the church has almost completely forgotten the biblical principles of marriage and divorce. How did the church forget these vital principles? We will look at this question in the next chapter.

FURTHER READING

Geniza Documents

Friedman, Mordechai. *A Jewish Marriage in Palestine: A Cairo Geniza Study.* Tel-Aviv: Tel-Aviv University, 1980. Collects and analyzes most of the mainstream rabbinic marriage contracts.

Olszowy-Schlanger, Judith. *Karaite Marriage Contracts from the Cairo Geniza: Legal Training and Community Life in Mediaeval Egypt and Palestine.* Leiden, Boston: E.J. Brill, 1998. This study does the same thing as Friedman's for marriage contracts of Karaite Jews. These are important because the Karaites were a back-to-the-Bible movement, so their contracts often reveal the biblical basis for older traditions.

Early English Marriage Services

Procter, Francis. *A History of the Book of Common Prayer: With a Rationale of Its Offices.* London: Macmillan, 1860. This is a very old book, but is still a standard work on which others are based.

Roman Women and Submission in the First Century

Fantham, Elaine, ed. *Women in the Classical World: Image and Text.* Oxford: Oxford University Press, 1995. Along with Sawyer's work, below, this is a good example of many books written on this subject by scholars of the classical world. Keener, Craig. *Paul, Women and Wives: Marriage and Women's Ministry in the Letters of Paul.* Peabody, Mass.: Hendrickson, 1992.

Keener is a New Testament scholar who is an expert on the Greco-Roman world.

Sawyer, Deborah F. *Women and Religion in the First Christian Centuries.* London: Routledge, 1996.

12

THE TEACHING THAT TIME FORGOT

Why did the church misunderstand Jesus so soon?

Almost all of the earliest church leaders, from the second century onward, believed that Jesus did not allow divorce and allowed separation only in the case of adultery. But as we have seen, anyone in the first century would have pointed out that this was a severe misunderstanding of what Jesus and Paul taught. So how could such a huge and drastic mistake have happened after such a short period of time?

SURVIVAL OF JUDAISM AFTER A.D.70

The first reason is the cataclysmic destruction of Jerusalem, which changed the whole world of Judaism and cut off Christianity from its Jewish roots. When the Romans defeated Jerusalem and destroyed the temple in A.D.70, much of the Jewish world of the New Testament was lost. Most of the Jewish leaders died during the siege, and Judaism was never the same again. The fact that rabbinic Judaism survived at all was remarkable; according to a traditional story, it was largely due to one man.

Johanan ben Zakkai was a Hillelite Pharisee who was an expert in both biblical interpretation and rabbinic law. He escaped from Jerusalem while it was besieged by pretending to be dead so that his disciples could carry him out in a coffin. The Roman guards were stopping everyone who tried to leave the city, but they let this small funeral party through, probably helped by a bribe. When they were safely out of sight, Johanan climbed out of the coffin, and instead of escaping, he went to the tent of the Roman commander, Vespasian. He told the commander that Scripture said that the one who conquered Jerusalem would be king, and therefore he prophesied that Vespasian would one day be emperor. Vespasian was very pleased with this and asked Johanan if he wanted anything. Johanan took his chance and requested that the city of Jamnia be given as a safe place for Jewish scholars, and Vespasian granted the request.

After the war, the surviving Jewish scholars gathered at Jamnia to establish a new center for rabbinic law. They called it a Sanhedrin after the religious parliament that had ruled in Jerusalem, though the Judaism that they presided over was very different from the Judaism of the New Testament era. A large number of Jewish groups virtually disappeared after A.D.70, including Sadducees, Herodians, Qumran Jews and Shammaite Pharisees. The only type of Jews who had any significant authority in this new age were Hillelite Pharisees like Johanan. Consequently the Jewish law from then on was interpreted in virtually every respect according to the traditions of the Hillelite school.

It is not surprising therefore that all divorces after this time were based on the Hillelite ground of "Any Cause," because even though its validity was disputed by Jesus and the Shammaites, as we saw in chapter five, the Hillelites were the only significant Jewish group to survive after A.D.70. It very quickly became the only type of Jewish divorce, and from then on it was not called an "Any Cause" divorce but simply "a divorce." The whole debate surrounding the legal phrase "Any Cause" and the Shammaite slogan "Nothing except 'sexual immorality'"—which had been as well-known in early first-century Judaism as the term "child support" is today—quickly disappeared from public consciousness. Within another couple of centuries these details had become obscure even to scholars.[1]

GENERATIONS DIVIDED BY LANGUAGE

It was not only the events of A.D.70 that led to this misunderstanding of the original legal debate: the evolution of language played a part as well. Nothing divides generations like language. One generation talks about things being "spiffing" or "swell" while another says "fab" or "hip"; then the next says they are "fantastic" or "excellent" and the next says they are "wicked" or "cool." One generation says, "We had a gay weekend," and the next says, "Don't tell anyone he's gay." A person with "learning disabilities" used to be called "educationally subnormal" and before that "mentally handicapped," but earlier still they were referred to by the technical medical term "imbecile." Someone from a previous generation could cause serious misunderstanding today by saying, "Isn't it wonderful that so many imbeciles are naturally gay?" when what they meant was that those with learning difficulties often have a very cheerful disposition.

Legal jargon changes too, though usually less quickly. For example, if you ask a group of people what a *co-respondent* is, only the older ones among them will remember that it is a legal term for the lover of someone being divorced for adultery. A few decades ago the newspapers regularly had stories about co-respondents, and thanks to human curiosity, these stories were popular reading. When divorce laws changed around the 1960s, the term all but disappeared from public consciousness, and in another few decades only social historians and readers of historical fiction will know the term. It will be as unknown as the term "Any Cause" was in the second century.

Another term that has changed its meaning completely is *intercourse.* What would you think of parents who told their daughter, "A young woman should avoid intercourse with men outside her social status"? Nowadays you might say they were libertine snobs, but in the 1800s they would be warning against *speaking* with unsuitable suitors.

The problem with shorthand phrases and assumed knowledge is that different readers have different assumptions. Imagine that you saw some demonstrators in Washington, D.C., with signs reading "Equality for women!" No one would expect the signs to read "We demand equality for women in pay and legal rights!"

Everyone knows that this is what the demonstrators actually mean; if the demonstration was reported in the newspapers, the journalist would not bother to spell it out. However if this demonstration occurred during the beginning of the twentieth century, the same slogan would mean something different: "We demand equality for women in education and voting rights!"

There would be no need, on either occasion, to spell out the whole slogan in a longer version, and it would be regarded as rather pedantic to do so. In both contexts it would be obvious what the short slogan meant, and the short version would be preferred over the longer one.

In the same way, when Matthew wrote his Gospel there was no need to spell out what "Any Cause" or "nothing except 'sexual immorality'" meant. A few years earlier, when Mark wrote his Gospel, he had not felt the need to include these phrases at all, because they would have been too obvious for his readers. As I said in chapter five, the insertion of these phrases in Mark would have seemed as pedantic as adding the words "alcoholic beverages" to the question "Is it lawful for a sixteen-year-old to drink?"

However, by the second century, when the legal phrases had been forgotten, the Pharisees' question to Jesus was understood as simply "Is it lawful to divorce one's wife for any cause?"—that is, "Is divorce *ever* lawful?" This was the "obvious" meaning at that time. No one spoke about "Any Cause" divorces anymore, not because they didn't exist but because they were the *only* type of divorce. Similarly today no one speaks about "co-respondents," not because they do not exist but because they are no longer mentioned in divorce cases. *Intercourse* now always means "sexual intercourse" and never means "speaking with." These examples show that changes in language are still happening and can cause misunderstandings over a couple of generations, even without the complete social upheaval that occurred when the Romans defeated Jerusalem in A.D.70.

MISSING PUNCTUATION

The church's misinterpretation of Jesus' teaching is further understandable because of the problem caused by translating the original Greek. Try to work out what the following words say:

PHARISEESCAMEUPTOHIMANDTESTEDHI
MBYASKINGISITLAWFULTODIVORCEONES
WIFEFORANYCAUSE

Like all New Testament manuscripts up to the third century, this lacks punctuation and is written completely in uppercase letters, without any spaces between the words. You can soon make out the words in the puzzle, but to illustrate how the translators could misunderstand it you have to write it down on a piece of paper, making sure that you add appropriate punctuation. Go on, have a go.

Probably you have written the sentence in the same way that the vast majority of Bible translations render the Greek:

> Pharisees came up to him and tested him by asking, "Is it lawful to divorce one's wife for any cause?"

This is a perfectly good translation of the Greek words, but it does not convey the correct meaning because some essential punctuation is missing. It is better to write it like this:

> Pharisees came up to him and tested him by asking, "Is it lawful to divorce one's wife for 'Any Cause'?"

The addition of quotation marks and capital letters to "Any Cause" is not strictly necessary, but it reminds the reader that this is a technical legal phrase. Without this reminder it is very easy to read the question as though the Pharisees were asking Jesus whether divorce is *ever* lawful. This mistake was already being made by the second century, because everyone except Jewish rabbis had already forgotten that the phrase "'Any Cause' divorce" ever existed.

GOD'S WORD CAN CROSS THE GENERATIONS

The words of Jesus had to cross many barriers between the first and second centuries. He spoke to first-century Jews in Aramaic; these words were then written down and abbreviated by the Gospel writers; and finally they were translated into Greek for a wider readership. The Christians of the second century were mainly Gentiles who were living under Roman law, so they had little knowledge of the synagogue or the Hebrew Old Testament. Thus Jesus' words had to cross the barriers of two or more generations, two completely dissimilar languages, and radically different social and legal cultures. So it is not surprising that second-century Christians occasionally misunderstood what he said.

When we read the Bible we face similar problems, though by now they have been multiplied many times. We are so far away from the time and culture of the original recipients of these words that sometimes it seems impossible for us to work out what the Holy Spirit was saying to them. Because of this, we often take short-cuts to understanding the text, so that when we read a passage of the Bible we tend to ask questions like these:

- What is the traditional interpretation of the church?

- What is the interpretation of my favorite teacher or preacher?

- What does this passage say to me right now, in plain English?

The question that we *should* ask ourselves is this:

- How did the original readers understand this?

This is a hard question to answer, because it involves looking at the text in its original language, in the context of the whole book and in the context of its culture and history. Often it cannot be answered with certainty, but we do have to make an effort, because this is the best chance we have for discovering what the author intended to communicate to his readers.

As Christians we have to assume that the Holy Spirit was able to convey truth accurately to the original readers in language and with concepts they would understand. We who come later have to do more work than they did in order to understand the same message, because we have to learn an ancient language and read it through the mindset of ancient thought-forms.

MODERN READERS HAVE TO WORK HARDER

As twenty-first-century readers we will always be at a disadvantage: we are not native readers of ancient Greek or Hebrew, so we have to rely on scholars to translate the texts for us. Also we are not living in a Roman city or in ancient Jewish culture, so we have to learn how people of that time thought and wrote and lived before we can be sure that we understand the translated texts.

For example, when the Bible speaks about "the God who searches the kidneys and heart" (Jer 20:12; Rev 2:23),[2] it means "God knows our emotions and thoughts." The ancients regarded the kidneys as the seat of emotions and the heart as the source of thoughts. If we did not understand these ancient concepts of human anatomy, these texts would give us a very strange idea about God's interest in our internal organs!

Another example: in the story of Zacchaeus in Luke 19, we can miss the whole point unless we have some background knowledge of ancient Jewish culture. We would not understand Jesus' love as expressed in this story unless we knew that tax collectors were the hated lackeys of the Roman occupation—something that we are not told in Scripture but learn from other historical sources. We would not understand the crowd's extreme consternation about Jesus' eating with sinners unless we knew about the fanatical concern most Jews had about purity laws—the details of which we know only from outside the New Testament. Zacchaeus kept much of his fortune, so Jesus told a parable about the wise use of money, but this parable makes no sense unless we know that ten minas (which older translations call "ten pounds") was a *huge* amount of money. None of this background knowledge is found in Scripture, but it is necessary for understanding Luke's message.

SCRIPTURE ALONE IS NOT ALWAYS ENOUGH

Some would say that Scripture contains everything we need to know—a principle that is sometimes misleadingly called *sola Scriptura* (Scripture alone). It is misleading because the real principle of *sola Scriptura* is that everything that is *necessary for salvation* can be found by a plain reading of Scripture, as we see in the definition in the Westminster Confession:

> The whole counsel of God, concerning all things necessary for his own glory, man's salvation, faith, and life, is either expressly set down in Scripture, or by good and necessary consequence may be deduced from Scripture.... All things in Scripture are not alike plain in themselves, nor alike clear unto all, yet those things which are necessary to be known, believed, and observed, for salvation, are so clearly propounded and opened in some place of Scripture or other,

that not only the learned, but the un-learned, in a due use of the ordinary means, may attain unto a sufficient under-standing of them.

Although divorce and remarriage are important topics, they are not necessary for salvation, and they do not therefore fall under the remit of *sola Scriptura* as envisioned by the Reform-ers. As the Westminster Confession says, there are many teachings (such as the way to deal with divorce and remarriage) that are "not plain in themselves, nor clear unto all."

We cannot approach Scripture without historical perspective. If we try to read it without taking into account how people thought at the time it was written, we will misunderstand a great deal of what God says to us. In this book we have often found that insights into ancient culture and language help us to understand what the Bible teaches about divorce and remarriage.

AN EXPLOSION OF INFORMATION

How much would you know about the two world wars if you had never had access to any news-papers, books or films about them? Even if your parents or grandparents told you about the wars, how much would you pass on to your children? Fortunately we do have detailed archives, and yet some people are still able to convince themselves that the Holocaust never happened. It seems paradoxical, but historians and archaeologists in the future will have a better chance of sorting out the truth than we do, when all available data have been analyzed carefully.

Similarly, we have a better chance of understanding the New Testament in its original context than did the second-century church fathers. We have a greater knowledge of the language and culture of the first century than they did, partly because we can have a more accurate perspective on the changes that happened by looking at them from a distance. We also know more because we benefit from centuries of work by scholars of language and history, and although many important documents have been lost, we have better access to ancient sources than did anyone living in the second century.

A library of a hundred books would have been a fabulous treasure for any ancient university, let alone an individual church scholar in the second century. Most churches did not even own a complete Bible, while most scholars were not wealthy enough to own even one book of their own. Even the best scholars would be unlikely to see more than a couple of hundred books in their whole lifetime. Nowadays most ministers have more books than this in their personal library. Anyone with access to the World Wide Web can read virtually every ancient source; I carry a copy of most ancient literature around with me on my pocket computer. The church fathers could not even dream of such riches.

These texts have been analyzed and reanalyzed by scholars for hundreds of years, and although scholars are still making significant discoveries (as this book has shown), we now have a very clear idea of the language and culture of the first century.

CONCLUSION: CROSSING THE GULF

We have seen that there was a huge gulf between the language and culture of New Testament times and the second-century church fathers, especially because of the destruction of Jerusalem and the complete change in Judaism at A.D.70. Even without this type of cataclysm, we have seen that today we are separated from our own ancestors by changes in language and culture as recently as twenty-five years ago.

But it still seems strange that the early church itself did not notice that its teaching had changed, and it is equally strange that modern scholars have not pointed out this change before. These questions, which are potentially embarrassing to church theologians and scholars alike, are addressed in the next chapter.

13

CONSPIRACY?

Why has no one explained all this before?

Much of the information in this book has been available to scholars for more than a century, and you might well be asking why the church has not reexamined its teaching on divorce and remarriage to take it into account. Was it simply due to incompetence and the inability to fit all the facts together? Or was there a conspiracy? Although one of the Dead Sea Scrolls was suppressed and the status quo of the church is a powerful consideration, I don't think there was a conspiracy—but you may disagree when you find out some of the facts.

REVEALING THE DEAD SEA SCROLLS

From the day they were discovered to the day of their full publication, the Dead Sea Scrolls were surrounded by mystery and intrigue. The delay in publication, caused by the length of time it took for scholars to complete the huge task of editing the documents, provoked rumors that they were being deliberately suppressed.

One such rumor suggested that the Vatican wanted to hide heretical details about Jesus, and another one said that some Jewish scholars were trying to hide embarrassing discoveries.

When the original scrolls were eventually put on public display in the specially built Shrine of the Book in Jerusalem, there was great excitement and the press was out in force, expecting to report scandalous revelations. A friend of mine who was working on one of the texts at that time told me that there was a huge commotion in the librarian's office as the journalists were asking questions, but none of them went to actually see any of the newly unveiled ancient documents. The scholars did not bother to attend either, because they already knew what the journalists were about to find out—there were no "suppressed" documents.

A SUPPRESSED DIVORCE DOCUMENT

So the conspiracy theories were proved to be baseless? Well, no—there was one exception. One of the Dead Sea Scrolls was deliberately concealed. It had been discovered, alongside other documents written in the early second century, at Murabba'at, a little distance from

the Qumran caves. One of the scholars responsible for publishing the Dead Sea Scrolls, J.T.
Milik, edited and published the Murabba'at
documents promptly, except for this particular
one, which he gave to another scholar, Jonas
Greenfield. Greenfield put the document in a
drawer, and although he mentioned it in a
couple of lectures, he refused to make the text
public.

After Greenfield's death the document passed
to a student of his, Ada Yardeni. She edited
and published it in 1995 without any translation
and with a limited circulation. It soon became
clear why Greenfield had kept it hidden: it was
a Jewish divorce certificate written by a woman.
Greenfield had been an expert on Jewish marriage law, and like many other Jews, he had
believed that first- and second-century Judaism
represented a golden age when the rabbinic
law was kept very faithfully—and rabbinic law,
of course, did not allow women to initiate a
divorce. This document had therefore been just
too embarrassing for him to publish.

After it was eventually published, there was a
heated scholarly squabble. Some scholars
proposed changing a few characters in the text
so that it would read as if it were a letter
written by a woman, in which she was simply

quoting the words of a divorce certificate that had been written by her former husband. Other scholars maintained that the text should be translated as it was, but this was confusing because it then read as if part of it was written by a man and part of it by a woman. My article in *Harvard Theological Review* ended this part of the debate, because I pointed out that if the document is simply translated literally, it is clearly a divorce certificate, written by a male scribe on behalf of a woman to her husband.

It is significant that the woman is not citing any particular fault by her husband and so she is not applying for a divorce on the Exodus 21:10 grounds of neglect. She appears instead to be basing her divorce on "Any Cause," even though this type of divorce was, strictly speaking, available only to men.

JEWISH DIVORCE CHANGED IN THE SECOND CENTURY

Greenfield had wanted to believe that in the first and second centuries rabbinic Judaism was identical to that of later orthodox Judaism. This document, written in the early second century, shows that on the contrary

Judaism was very much in transition throughout this period, particularly with regard to divorce and remarriage. By the early second century, the "Any Cause" divorce had taken over to such an extent that the biblical divorces for neglect, which early-first-century Judaism allowed women to initiate, had already been forgotten, even by Jewish scribes.

Perhaps my assessment of Greenfield's delay in publication is unfair, because he may have still been studying the document, but this incident highlights the fact that sometimes a key piece of knowledge can be withheld by someone in an effort to prevent a dearly held belief's being shown to be wrong. Both Judaism and the Christian church can be equally guilty of ignoring important findings in order to maintain the status quo.

In spite of the above, I think the major reason the church has not collated all this information accurately is confusion rather than conspiracy, because changes in society during the life of the early church led it to emphasize a different message in Jesus' words.

A WORLD DOMINATED BY SEX

By the second century, the Roman world had become dominated by sex: husbands and wives both had homosexual and heterosexual lovers; prostitutes not only were accepted but were a normal part of cultured life; at a meal, the host was expected to provide professional sexual entertainment, called the "after dinners"; and extramarital affairs were made easier by the widespread use of primitive, though effective, contraception (and when this failed, the baby was killed). Sex had become cheapened into a commodity, and sexual immorality was such an all-pervasive vice that even marital sex became tainted. The sexual act became despised and feared by the church as a source of corruption and spiritual disease, and the church ended up being suspicious of even conjugal relations within marriage.

Many religious groups reacted against this trend by taking up a directly opposite stance—that is, by preaching abstinence from all unnecessary sexual contact.

Some Jewish groups had already started to think this way in the first century. We know that the Dead Sea community kept sexual contact to a minimum, and there were probably other smaller Jewish groups who did the same. Some of the Corinthian converts seem to have been influenced by this type of group, because they ask Paul what he thinks about the saying "It is good for a man not to have sexual relations with a woman" (1 Cor 7:1). Paul rejects this teaching on the standard Jewish grounds that sex is a good and necessary component of any marriage (1 Cor 7:2-5).

By the second century many more Jews had become suspicious of sex. No pious Jew could actually reject sex completely, since having children was compulsory, but they could refrain from it after they had children. The only unmarried rabbi we know of, R. Ben Assi, lived in the second century. He had been married (so he had fulfilled his religious duty), but he refused to get remarried, even though everyone expected him to do so. He defended himself by saying that he was married to the Scriptures and was too busy. His potential father-in-law, Akiva, was probably sympathetic because, although he was married, he had spent fourteen years away from his wife in order to study at the rabbinic academy in Jamnia.

These two second-century rabbis were members of an ascetic movement that avoided unnecessary sexual relations and other activities in pursuit of religious experiences by means of meditation. Very few details about this movement survive because it was suppressed by mainstream rabbis, but the evidence we do have suggests that there was a strong underground movement within second-century Judaism which sought to avoid sexual activity, despite the Jewish law that everyone should have children.

CHURCH FEARS ABOUT SEX

The Christian church did not have a similar law about having children to give it a positive message about sex within marriage, so there was nothing to inhibit the ascetic movement. A large proportion of Christians started to assume that sex was evil, or at least that it was a route toward evil and something to avoid, so although marriage was still celebrated, the avoidance of marriage was highly recommended. If a widow or widower remarried, it was regarded as evidence of lasciviousness, since they had already done their sexual duty by being married before; it was felt to be a willful reversal of God's decision to end a period of sexual relations.

Tertullian was a Christian teacher at the end of the second century who wrote books on the subject of marriage and open letters to his wife about remarriage, so we have a very detailed knowledge of what he believed on these subjects. He told his wife that if he died she should not get remarried, because although this would not be sinful, it would not be God's will.

> When, through the will of God, the husband is deceased, the marriage likewise, by the will of God, deceases. Why should you restore what God has put an end to? ... For even if you do not "sin" in re-marrying, still he says "pressure of the flesh ensues." Wherefore, so far as we can, let us love the opportunity of continence.[1]

The church gradually elevated celibacy higher and higher until, by the ninth century, the Roman church had decided that priests must be unmarried, that celibacy within marriage was a pious choice and that sexual relations without the goal of having children were sinful. This trend, which started in the second century, was largely based on the misunderstanding that both Jesus and Paul taught that virginity was superior to the married state and that re-marriage was always impious and often sinful.

NEW TEACHING FOR A NEW AGE

In the context of this emphasis against sex, it was natural that the second-century church would assume that Jesus taught remarriage was equivalent to sexual immorality and would not be surprised when he appeared to identify remarriage with "adultery." Even if the earliest of the church fathers had realized that their interpretation, or at least their emphasis of Jesus' words, was different from that of first-century believers, undoubtedly they would have considered their own teaching to be correct for their time.

What was more difficult to explain was why their teaching was so different from the Old Testament. They had to justify why Moses said that God allowed divorce and remarriage when Jesus seemed to condemn them both in the strongest language.

Most of the early church fathers explained it by simply saying that the Old Testament was for then and Jesus' teaching was for now. Others were uneasy with this explanation because it made God appear to have changed his mind, and they tried to come up with other reasons. For example, Ptolemaeus (in the late second century) said that Moses deliberately misrepresented God's commands, and Origen (in the early third century) said that Moses simply made up the law about divorce to supply what was lacking in God's law. Despite their embarrassment, however, the church fathers were convinced that Jesus did reject the Old Testament laws.

TRADITION VERSUS SCRIPTURE

In some branches of the Christian church, one of the main ways of evaluating whether an interpretation of Scripture is correct is to measure it against the interpretations of the church fathers—though no one would want to elevate the traditions of former church leaders above Scripture itself. But although it is certainly true that the commentaries of the fathers are important for their insights and their knowledge of ancient traditions, this is not a guarantee that their interpretations are always correct.

In fact very few people today would defend some of the ways they interpreted Scripture. For example, almost all the early church fathers taught that there was no forgiveness for those who gave in to torture by pagan persecutors and cursed Christ to escape death. Since persecution was such a major problem for them, we can understand *why* they interpreted texts such as Hebrews 10:26 in this way, but most people would now explain these texts as a condemnation of those who *willfully* reject Christ, rather than those who break under torture.

DISPUTES ABOUT DOCTRINES

Arguments over doctrine have featured throughout the history of the church. Early disputes included different interpretations about the Trinity and the divinity of Christ. Conflicts over other things, such as the date of Easter and the status of the Holy Spirit, resulted in the permanent division between the Eastern and Western churches. Later disputes, including those over the authority of the pope and other doctrines such as indulgences (which were later changed during the Catholic Church's internal reformation), resulted in the Catholic-Protestant split. In more recent times, the church has been split over the status of scientific discoveries, the gifts of the Spirit, women's ministry and a host of other issues.

These conflicts have resulted in excommunication, torture, death and even wars. We might wish that the Holy Spirit would preserve us from such discord by making Scripture more plain or by inspiring the scholars on both sides to agree with each other, but God does not work in this way. He gives us intelligence to think about difficult doctrines and then expects us to listen to each other in humility and in a desire to find the truth. But human nature, being what it is, we find it difficult to review time-worn beliefs, even when new insights are clearly significant or when historical discoveries uncover information that had been lost.

DISCOVERIES IGNORED BY THEOLOGIANS

Most of the historical data presented in this book have been known to Christian scholars for the last 150 years, but theologians have failed to apply the information to the doctrine of marriage and divorce. Virtually every significant commentary on Matthew since 1850 mentions the dispute between the Hillelites and the Shammaites. Before then, the information had been available in the large volumes of rabbinic law that were well known to Jews, though not to Christians.

Although the full significance of these rabbinic texts was not clear until the discovery of the Dead Sea Scrolls and other documents from the Judean desert, the clues were there and could have been correctly applied if there had been a willingness to look at the question dispassionately. Even Henry Alford, who wrote his Greek Testament commentary on Matthew in 1849, pointed out that Josephus divorced his wife on the grounds of "Any Cause" and that Jesus took part in a debate between the Hillelites and Shammaites on this issue.[2]

There is actually a very good reason the church has not reassessed its teaching about divorce and remarriage: *no* church doctrine should change. Preserving the status quo in this case is normally assumed to be the best policy, because God does not change and his truth does not change. Church doctrine should not be allowed to blow one way and then the other simply because society has changed. In fact, the purpose of this book has not been to argue for a new interpretation of Scripture but for an *old* one, that is, the interpretation of the hearers and readers of the words of Jesus and Paul in the first century.

CONCLUSION: REVERSING THE CHANGE IN CHURCH DOCTRINE

It must be admitted that changes in society *have* been an incentive for this study. Although I've pursued the subject with the rigor and discipline of a scholar, my thoughts have often dwelt on actual abuse within Christian marriages and the misery that is produced by the church's teaching. I don't think that marital abuse has increased in this generation, but the increasing openness of society means that we now hear much more about it, and church teaching has been brought into disrepute as a result.

Changes in society were also the incentive for the church fathers to accept a different interpretation of Jesus' teaching, because they needed a way to steer the church away from the hedonistic lifestyles of the second century. Like them, we are in danger of finding only what we want to find in the words of the New Testament, so we must make sure we listen to the Holy Spirit as well as to the scholars.

Jesus promised that the Holy Spirit would lead us into all truth, but this depends on our listening to him. We know that the Holy Spirit will not force us to hear the truth—theologians and scholars have not preserved the church from divisions or even wars in the past—so we must be willing to listen to each other and, most of all, to listen to Scripture. We should use our God-given intelligence while we seek to understand and apply his Word, and we should pray for God to point out the truth to us. And of course, we should be prepared to admit that we might be wrong.

FURTHER READING

Dead Sea Scrolls and Conspiracies

Betz, Otto, and Rainer Riesner. *Jesus, Qumran and the Vatican.* New York: Crossroad, 1994. Debunks the conspiracy theories once for all.

Stegemann, Hartmut. *The Library of Qumran.* Grand Rapids: Eerdmans, 1998. A good overview of the findings and the conclusions we can draw from them.

The Suppressed Divorce Certificate

Instone-Brewer, David. "Jewish Women Divorcing Their Husbands in Early Judaism: The Background to Papyrus Sie'elim 13." *Harvard Theological Review* 92 (1999):349-57. This article corrected previous translations, which were based on an emended version of this contract, and discusses the Jewish divorce laws of the second century.

First- and Second-Century Views on Sex and Feminism

Deming, Will. *Paul on Marriage and Celibacy: The Hellenistic Background of 1 Corinthians 7.* Cambridge: Cambridge University Press, 1995. Looks at asceticism mainly among Greek philosophers but also the early church fathers.

Keener, Craig. "Marriage, Divorce and Adultery." In *Dictionary of the Later New Testament and Its Developments,* ed. Ralph P. Martin and Peter H. Davids. Downers Grove, Ill.: InterVarsity Press, 1997. Traces the start of asceticism in the church to the *Shepherd of Hermas* in the second half of the second century, though Hermas is probably no more than the first enthusiastic exponent of it.

Winter, Bruce. "The 'New' Roman Wife and 1 Timothy 2:9-15: The Search for a Sitz im Leben." *Tyndale Bulletin* 51 (2000):283-92. Looks at feminism in the first century.

14

WHAT SHOULD THE CHURCH DO NOW?

Putting biblical principles into practice.

If you have come straight here without reading the previous chapters, please let me encourage you to go back and do so; otherwise you will find out the book's conclusions, but you will not know about its scriptural foundations. The purpose of this book has been to give you information that will help you to make up your own mind about the Bible's teaching, and the purpose of this chapter is to remind you what we have found out so as to put it together as a set of biblical principles.

SUMMARY OF THIS BOOK

Chapter one reviewed the church's traditional teaching on divorce and remarriage, which many pastors have found to be unworkable. It also pointed out that sometimes what we *think* is in the Bible is not actually there.

Chapter two showed us that God's ideal for marriage is a loving, lifetime relationship, yet we also saw that the Old Testament is very practical with regard to the sin of marriage breakup. In the ancient Near East, women could be abandoned by their husbands and then reclaimed by them later. This meant they were never free to find another husband to help bring up the children. God dealt with this problem in Israel by commanding that a husband who left his wife must give her a divorce certificate, which gave her the right to remarry.

In *chapter three* we found that God himself is a divorcee. The Old Testament prophets described God's relationship with Israel as if it was a marriage: when Israel worshiped other gods, she was likened to an unfaithful wife; she broke all her marriage vows while God continued to clothe, feed and love her faithfully. We saw that the prophets did not regard divorce itself as an evil act but considered the breaking of marriage vows as the sin that breaks up the marriage. God was the victim in his relationship with Israel and was therefore entitled to decide when the marriage was over. God's divorce also gave us an insight into the way he feels about divorce: he hates it because it means that promises in the marriage contract have been broken (Mal 2:14-16).

Chapter four reminded us that Jesus affirmed the teaching of the Old Testament, so we cannot simply reject the moral principles we find there. Further, in *chapter five,* we saw that he criticized the Pharisees for abandoning Old Testament teaching when they introduced the new groundless type of divorce named "Any Cause." Jesus defended the plain meaning of the Old Testament phrase "a cause of sexual immorality," which he (and the Shammaites) said meant "nothing except 'sexual immorality,'" that is, adultery. Jesus also emphasized that divorce is never compulsory, even if adultery has taken place, and that believers should only divorce someone who is "hardhearted"—stubbornly unrepentant, as Israel was.

In *chapter six* we saw that Paul was equally critical of groundless divorces. He told believers that they should not use the Roman divorce-by-separation and if they had already separated they should try if possible to reconcile and remarry their partner. On the other hand, if someone had divorced *them,* Paul recognized that there wasn't anything they could do about it, so in this case he said they were "not enslaved" (which is what any divorce certificate would have told them). He accepted that being divorced against your will could be regarded as a valid biblical divorce on the grounds of neglect.

Many people believe that marriage lasts till death, whether or not the former spouses think they are divorced. *Chapter seven* looked at this point of view in the light of the Bible and found no basis for this interpretation. Many people also teach that a Christian should never divorce, even in cases of abuse, but *chapter eight* pointed out that the Old Testament law, which gave a neglected or abused partner the right to a divorce, was not repealed by Jesus and that Paul assumed that it still applied.

What about remarriage after divorce? The New Testament is remarkably vague on this important issue, but *chapter nine* pointed out that first-century believers would have had no uncertainty because the right to remarry was taken for granted. It was a legal right that was recorded in all Jewish divorce certificates, and in Roman law remarriage was actually a legal *duty.* Christians would no doubt have avoided remarriage if they had been told to, but they would have needed a very clear directive because to do so would have meant breaking the law. Neither Paul nor Jesus gave this directive, however, and although Paul never actually said "A divorcee may remarry," we saw that some of his teaching assumed that remarriage was allowed for Christians.

In *chapter ten* we looked at the difficult situation of those who have remarried after an invalid divorce. Jesus said this type of remarriage is like adultery, but we concluded that he did not want remarried couples to get divorced any more than he wants us to treat a foul-tempered outburst as if it were literally murder or treat lustful thinking as though this were literally adultery. We also found that when Paul told abandoned believers that they could remarry because "God has called you to peace," he was using legal jargon that meant "This case is decided on pragmatic grounds." Even guilty partners can remarry, because God is able to forgive someone who repents of an invalid divorce that cannot be reconciled without breaking up another marriage.

Chapter eleven showed that our modern wedding service still retains the vows that originated from Exodus 21. We can trace the wording in the earliest English marriage service back to both Jewish marriage contracts and Ephesians 5:28-29, where "love, honor and cherish" (and other variations) originate. I also recounted my experience of using a service of repentance before re-marrying divorcees.

Why was Jesus' teaching misunderstood so soon? *Chapter twelve* showed that the de-struction of the temple in A.D.70 marked a huge shift in the culture and theology of Judaism, as well as sealing the rift between Christians and Jews. This meant that Chris-tians no longer understood the rabbinic legal phrases that Jesus and Paul used like "Any Cause" and "God has called you to peace."

Chapter thirteen asked why it has taken so long to realize that this misunderstanding had occurred and concluded that it is due to confusion rather than a conspiracy. The stand that the second-century church took against sexual immorality made their new emphasis against remarriage (a misinterpre-tation of Jesus' teaching) seem normal. Once this new interpretation had become church doctrine it was difficult for the church to come to terms with the fact that a misunderstanding had taken place.

SIMILAR CONCLUSIONS BY THE REFORMERS WITHOUT THE RECENT DISCOVERIES

This book has uncovered several pieces of information that are needed to help us understand what the Bible means:

- The need for a divorce certificate in Moses' law is explained by the fact that a husband in the ancient Near East had the right to reclaim a wife he had abandoned.

- The question that the Pharisees asked Jesus makes sense when we know about the new "Any Cause" divorces of that time.

- Jesus' silence about the other Old Testament grounds for divorce is unsurprising when we find that all Jews in Jesus' day accepted their validity.

- Paul's teaching about "separation" speaks to the Roman practice of divorce-by-separation.

- The lack of clear teaching about remarriage in the New Testament has to be seen in the light of the legal right and duty to re-marry that existed in the first century.

Although this new information is important for demonstrating what the text means, we are still able to understand the text correctly without it. When the Reformers read the Bible with relatively independent minds, they came to many of the same conclusions that this new evidence leads us to.

Erasmus realized that marriage was not a "sacrament" that continued till death despite divorce, and therefore he allowed remarriage after divorce for adultery or abandonment by an unbeliever. All the major Reformers agreed with his conclusions, and Martin Luther also allowed divorce for abandonment by a believer. Other Reformers, such as Ulrich Zwingli and Heinrich Bullinger, said that the New Testament does not list all the grounds for divorce, so they could allow other grounds such as abuse. Thomas Cranmer wanted to base Anglican theology on his *Reformatio Legum Ecclesiasticarum,* which allowed divorce and remarriage after adultery, desertion, prolonged absence, mortal hatred or cruelty, but this reform was prevented by Elizabeth I.

MODERN THEOLOGIANS WITH SIMILAR CONCLUSIONS

Many modern theologians have come to conclusions that are similar to those in this book, though they have usually admitted that they did not have sufficient biblical support for them. They have based their conclusions on the *principles* in the Bible rather than the details in these difficult texts on divorce and remarriage. Here are some of the more successful attempts at biblical exegesis:

- David Atkinson's *To Have and to Hold: The Marriage Covenant and the Discipline of Divorce* (London: Collins, 1979) offers a very good understanding of biblical marriage as a contract.

- William F. Luck, in *Divorce and Remarriage: Recovering the Biblical View* (San Francisco: Harper & Row, 1987), recognizes the importance of Exodus 21:10-11 but fails to follow this text into the New Testament.

- Craig Keener's *... And Marries Another: Divorce and Remarriage in the Teaching of the New Testament* (Peabody, Mass.: Hendrickson, 1991) acknowledges Paul's references to Roman divorce-by-separation and points out most of the Jewish background to the Gospel accounts.

- Bernard Haring, a Catholic priest and lecturer in moral theology, wrote the very honest *No Way Out? Pastoral Care of the Divorced and Remarried* (Slough, U.K.: St Paul, 1989) while dying of cancer. He commends the Greek Orthodox theology of allowing divorce and remarriage after a *marriage* has died rather than waiting for a former partner to die.

Most pastoral theologians have concluded on pragmatic grounds that we must allow divorce for abandonment and cruelty, and most also include emotional and material neglect as valid grounds for divorce. They also point out that it is unjust to punish an innocent partner in the same way as a partner who broke up a marriage by preventing both of them from remarrying until their first spouse dies. Most of them would add that even the guilty partner should be allowed to remarry after repentance, because otherwise the church would have to decide who is "innocent" and would be making marriage breakup into an unforgivable sin.

BIBLICAL PRINCIPLES AND CHURCH POLICY

These conclusions by pastoral theologians, which until now were not often based on Scripture, are very similar to the principles we have discovered in the Bible:

1. Marriage is a lifetime contract between two partners, and marriage vows are the stipulations of this contract.

2. Both partners vow to provide material support and physical affection and to be sexually faithful to each other.

3. If one partner breaks a marriage vow, the other has the right to decide either to end the marriage with a divorce or to carry on.

4. Divorce should take place only if vows have been broken, and it is always sinful to break these vows.

5. Jesus adds the caveat that we should forgive an erring partner unless they break their vows continuously or without repentance.

6.   Paul adds the caveat that if a divorce takes place without citing broken vows, remarriage to another is allowed only if reconciliation is impossible.

The overriding principle in all these is that the wronged partner must be able to choose. They must be able to decide whether to regard the marriage contract as broken or whether to persevere with it. And if they have been divorced against their will in a civil court, they should be able to decide whether to attempt a reconciliation.

On the basis of these principles a church might adopt the following set of policies:

1.   The biblical grounds for divorce are adultery, neglect and abuse, any of which is equivalent to broken marriage vows.

2.   No one should initiate a divorce unless their partner is guilty of repeatedly or unrepentantly breaking their marriage vows.

3.   No one should separate from their marriage partner without intending to divorce them.

4.   If someone has divorced or separated without biblical grounds, they should at-

tempt a reconciliation with their former partner.

5. Remarriage is allowed in church for any divorcee after a service of repentance, unless they have divorced a wronged partner who wants to be reconciled.

CONTRADICTIONS IN PRESENT CHURCH POLICY

Most churches have contradictions in their policies with regard to divorce in that they allow divorce for adultery but not for attempted murder. And when they do allow divorce, this is actually no more than separation, because they do not allow remarriage. This is contrary to Paul's teaching that those who are married should live together and care for each other (1 Cor 7:3-5, 33-34). In effect, this teaching has invented a new state somewhere between married and single that Augustine named "separation from house and hearth" *(a mensa et thoro)*. Although the majority of the Reformers rejected this concept, most Protestant churches implicitly accept it when they allow (or encourage) someone to separate from a partner without divorcing him or her.

This new concept of "separation without divorce" results in a situation where people are forced to live singly without being able to remarry. This bring us full circle, back to the situation that existed before the law of Moses, in which a husband could abandon a wife without giving her the freedom to remarry—a situation that God remedied by commanding that the woman should be given a divorce certificate.

Among all the hundreds of different combinations of possible ways to interpret the biblical teaching on divorce and remarriage, I have found only two that are fully coherent without any internal contradictions and that can be said to be based on Scripture. The first says that the New Testament does not allow divorce at all because marriage lasts till death and Jesus and Paul allowed exceptions to this rule only because they were necessitated by Jewish and Greco-Roman law. Jesus allowed divorce after adultery because for the Jews it was compulsory to divorce after a wife's adultery. Likewise, Paul made an exception in the case of separation by an unbeliever, because the Greco-Roman world regarded separation as divorce. When this teaching is applied to our society, it means that believers should never divorce, and if they are divorced against their will, they cannot remarry.

This view is best represented by William A. Heth and Gordon J. Wenham in *Jesus and Divorce,* though they do not include the explanation for Paul's exception. It is based on the assumption that Jewish believers could be forced to divorce adulterous partners, but this is erroneous because there was no ruling body with the power to enforce such a command. Jewish society had many religious authorities (Pharisee, Sadducee, Essene, etc.) but none of them could impose their will—except by excommunicating someone from their own synagogue.

The only other coherent solution is the one that first-century believers would have inferred from the New Testament: that divorce is allowed only for the victim of broken marriage vows and that the right to remarriage is implicit in any divorce. In our society this would mean that a believer should divorce only if they have biblical grounds (even if these grounds are not named as the legal basis for their divorce) and that all divorcees may remarry unless their wronged ex-partner wants a reconciliation.

HOW CAN WE APPLY THESE FINDINGS?

What can we do with the results of this study? In many churches with a strong tradition, the answer will be, Very little. The ship of the church is too large and its canon law is too well established for it to change course now, even if a huge number of people are leaning on the rudder. Smaller, younger denominations have a better chance to change direction and to return to a first-century interpretation of the Bible.

Reasserting these principles is made possible by the remarkable fact that the Holy Spirit has preserved the biblical marriage vows in the wedding services of virtually every Christian denomination. It is amazing that, despite all the changes in church theology with regard to marriage and divorce, the wording of our wedding services has remained fairly constant, so that church practice has continued to be centered on the original biblical marriage vows. When we marry, we all still promise to love, nourish, cherish and be faithful to each other. Although the exact wording varies in different marriage services (as it did in New Testament times), the principles of the biblical marriage have remained intact. The fact that all Christian marriages are already based on these biblical vows makes it much easier to reintroduce the concept of divorce based on broken marriage vows.

Individual churches will approach this in different ways. Some will merely teach their flock that this is what believers *should* do, while others will attempt to back up the teaching with some kind of church discipline, such as excommunication or temporary exclusion from Communion, or by refusing to remarry those who divorce their partner without biblical grounds. I'd like to think that churches will concentrate less on discipline and more on pastoral counseling.

Marriage counseling is often hampered by the lack of a coherent biblical approach to divorce and remarriage. In the light of this study a Christian counselor can say with confidence that believers do have grounds for divorce in cases of adultery, abuse or neglect but that Jesus asks us to forgive partners who repent after breaking their vows. Jesus allows us to divorce a "hardhearted" partner, but neither he nor Paul chose to define how much neglect is too much—unlike the rabbis, who defined the minimum amount of food, clothing and con-jugal love that was due.

This biblical teaching gives people who are suffering within marriages both an encourage-ment to persevere and a safety net when they find they cannot cope with it any more. They can, if necessary, divorce their "hard-hearted" partner in the knowledge that God himself was forced down this route when Is-rael hardheartedly broke her marriage vows to him. The divorce that God went through brought much pain and suffering, according to the prophets, and no one expects divorce to bring happiness, but sometimes divorce is necessary in order to end the sinfulness of repeated and unrepentant breaking of marriage vows. Divorce is never good, but sometimes it is the only way to end the evil of a broken marriage.

CONCLUSION: PRINCIPLES FOR REAL LIFE

We can now understand what Jesus and Paul were saying to their listeners about divorce and remarriage, which means that we can now understand what God is saying to us. We have found that the New Testament teaching is both practical and caring. God's love reaches out to those who are struggling in broken marriages, to the wronged divorcee and also to the sinners who have broken their marriage vows and repented.

We have found a set of biblical principles that some denominations will be able to apply in their church practice and that all churches will find useful in marriage counseling. Applying these principles will not always be easy, because principles are not the same as rules and no two marriages are the same. Some of the practical problems that arise are illustrated by the real-life situations addressed in the next chapter.

FURTHER READING

Teaching of the Reformers

Instone-Brewer, David. *Divorce and Remarriage in the Bible.* Grand Rapids: Eerdmans, 2002. The second half of chapter 9, "History of Divorce," examines the different teachings of the Reformers, especially Erasmus and Luther.

Smith, David L. "Divorce and Remarriage from the Early Church to John Wesley." *Trinity Journal* n.s., 11 (1990):131-42. Covers more

Reformers, including John Calvin, William Tyndale and Thomas Cranmer.

Biblical Basis for Divorce for Abuse

Adams, Jay. *Marriage, Divorce and Remarriage in the Bible.* Phillipsburg, N.J.: Presbyterian & Reformed, 1980. Argues for divorce for abandonment by believers because they are acting like nonbelievers.

Clark, Stephen. *Putting Asunder: Divorce and Remarriage in Biblical and Pastoral Perspective.* Bridgend, U.K.: Brynterion, 1999. Argues that believers who act against the interest of the marriage can be divorced because they act like nonbelievers who don't want the marriage to continue (as in 1 Cor 7:12-13).

Instone-Brewer, David. *Divorce and Remarriage in the Bible.* Grand Rapids: Eerdmans, 2002. Chapter 10, "Modern Reinterpretations," examines the multitude of different ways in which the biblical texts have been interpreted.

15

DEAR PASTOR...

Real-life problems from my mailbox.

I have a parish of hundreds of thousands through a very busy website (www.Divorce-Re marriage.com). I put most of my work on the site as I write it; about a thousand people visit it per week, and a few of them email me. This came yesterday from an American man:

When I found your website I cried (for joy) and I just wanted to thank you. I was in a church that taught there was no reason to get divorced, except perhaps adultery. In my marriage, I was in a pervasive emotionally abusive situation, and the counsel of my Christian friends was to "hang in there." Finally, I had a dream where I was standing before God and I had done something violent to end the abuse. God asked me a question: "Why did you not just leave?" It was then that I knew I needed to get out of my marriage, regardless of what my church taught and what my friends said. They all asked me what was the biblical basis of my divorce, as I was abused but they did not see that as a valid reason...

I can now point them to your website for a scholarly and very credible explanation of my position. As you say, the whole position on marriage and divorce is made coherent by understanding the Jewish context. I ordered three copies of your book, one for me, one for my pastor, and one for my psychological counselor. I thank God that you have had the courage to speak the truth in love as you understand it. Praise God!

A British woman emailed me a few weeks ago:

> Just came across your web pages completely by accident whilst researching into the effects of divorce on pensions! As a Christian and an active member of a parochial church council (PCC), my decision to divorce my abusive husband after six and a half years was not taken lightly and only after years of soul-searching, prayer and finally desperation as I clambered back from depression and breakdown. I knew that God did not intend for me to suffer as I was suffering yet could find no other answer. I concluded that the biblical ideal of marriage could only be attained if both parties were aiming for the same goal and could not believe that I was expected to continue living in this manner despite evi-

dence to the contrary. A few months prior to making my decision, I consulted my parish rector and discussed my anguish at length, and he did persuade me to try to make it work.

Following my decision, I sent a letter of resignation to the PCC explaining that due to my situation, I no longer felt it appropriate to continue serving on the council and that I was having problems dealing with the compromising of my faith. I received a letter thanking me for my work over the years and wishing me luck in the future. No member of my church has contacted me since, leaving me with an even greater feeling of failure and sin. I have felt unable to walk into my church since and have not done so.

THE THEORY IS GOOD, BUT DOES IT WORK?

I have heard many stories like these of divorcees who have felt let down by their church just when they need its help most. A huge number of people are hurt and harmed during the course of their marriage, but we will never know exactly how many because often they suffer in secret. In the past women were the victims of broken marriage vows more often than men, but things are now equalizing. Both men and women commit adultery, and both men and women are abusive or neglectful, though men are much more likely to be violent.

The teaching of the church has compounded much of this hurt rather than alleviating it. Victims of continuing abuse have been told that they must stay married, and if they do get divorced, they have been told that they cannot remarry until their former partner has died. And sometimes those who have divorced and remarried are told by their church that they must now divorce their new spouse because in God's eyes they are still married to the person who abused or neglected them. Thus the church makes them a victim for a second time.

Most of my work on divorce and remarriage was done after I left the church pastorate to become a research fellow of an academic institution. While my mind wandered freely among the academic towers of Cambridge, my feet were kept firmly on the ground by a wide circle of church contacts and by e-mails like those in this chapter. The questions people asked often forced me to face up to practical implications of my studies, which I had not considered. These e-mails became, for me, a test by which my work could be judged, because if my interpretation of Scripture is correct, I would also expect it to be practical in pastoral situations. Whether my work has passed this test is for you to judge as you read these e-mails over my shoulder and see my replies.

FROM A WOMAN WHO STAYED WITH HER ABUSIVE HUSBAND

It has always been more important to me not to sin than to accommodate happiness in my life. Well, not always, or else I wouldn't have ended up in this situation in the first place, but it did at least become the most important eventually. Because of that, I wouldn't divorce. But this stance left me with an even bigger problem. My husband learned that he could do just about anything and I would take it because of my beliefs, and he did. All the way from beatings to going just to the line and stopping in other activities. He's entertained thoughts of at least three girls, dated one ... and let me know it was happening. I think my parents concluded that I was probably dropped on my head when I was little.... Why else would I be so ... stupid! ... to stay with a man who did these things.

I must tell you, your work on divorce and remarriage has got to be the best I've ever seen, and I've read a lot. Your writings aren't unusual in the position you take as much, as many have offered a similar perspective, but it's almost always based on "God doesn't want you to suffer" or "Common sense says..." It seemed to me that was really only looking for loopholes in God's Word. But the more I read in your writings, the more I realized that because we don't understand this issue, many people sincerely wanting to follow God have ended up in bondage to their own good intentions. Your writings are remarkable. It's going to take me a little time to reposition myself from my old ways of thinking, but ... I'm very grateful to you for presenting a truly biblical perspective on this issue, based on solid objective truth and not an emotional plea for "there must be some way out." God's blessings.

Reply: I'm so pleased that you wanted to follow Jesus' command, even when it was difficult. As you realize, I've concluded that the church has made things much more difficult for you than they need be. God loves you and knows that you are a victim, as well as knowing the ways in which you may perhaps have contributed to this breakdown. You are right that some Bible teachers appear to be looking for loopholes in the Bible's teaching—to find a "fair" solution—but please don't look down on them for doing this. They are trying to find a way to hold on to God's Word at the same time as holding on to the fact of God's love. I am fortunate to have found the key to understanding these texts, but good theologians, like Luther, have instinctively come to the same conclusions without being able to justify them fully.

God be with you as you seek his will at this time.

FROM A WOMAN IN A LOVELESS MARRIAGE

I have a question on my divorce and would like to know the biblical standpoint on it, being a born-again Christian (albeit backslidden).

When you say "They affirmed the ground for divorce in Deut 24:1 (adultery) and the other grounds for divorce in Ex 21:10f (neglect of material support and physical affection)," can I assume that the neglect of physical affection can also mean nonregular consummation of that marriage? I have been torturing myself for ages that I had no right to seek a divorce despite ten years of virtually total "neglect" in our marriage. By the age of thirty-one I felt I had given him enough time and chance to try and do something about it.

Reply: This issue is one of the most difficult things about the passage in Exodus 21:10-11, because there are so many possible reasons for refusing conjugal activity within marriage. When passions cool, the act of love can become boring or even disgusting for some people, and who can allocate blame for lack of libido? Physical frailty creeps up unequally sometimes, leaving one partner wanting no more than a cuddle while leaving the other one frustrated. Sometimes medical and emotional problems intervene. Frequently these problems can be sorted out by talking them through—though I realize that it's hard to discuss these things—and often a counselor is helpful. The Bible speaks in plain language on these issues, and Paul is quite blunt! So we should not treat sexual problems as unimportant or unspiritual.

Without knowing you and your former husband personally, it is impossible to know if you can divorce him for neglect of physical affection, and even if I did know you these things are not open to public scrutiny! It certainly sounds from what you say that your husband was not honoring his debt of love (as Paul puts it in 1 Cor 7:3-5), and it sounds as though you gave him many opportunities to change his ways. If you honestly conclude that your husband has unjustifiably denied you your right to sexual relations and refuses to change, then it sounds as though you do have biblical grounds for divorce—but only you and God know.

ABOUT A FOOLISH MARRIAGE

> My daughter married a man that she did not love. She is not sure why she married him other than she was in love with the idea of the wedding. She has stayed married for four years, and love for him has never grown. She is miserable, and her unhappiness is wearing heavy on her emotional and physical health. She needs spiritual direction. Could you please help?

Reply: This is a very sad situation, but I can't see that there is any biblical "way out" for her because the promises that your daughter made are valid, even if they were made unthinkingly or for foolish reasons. Catholic theologians might allow annulment of a marriage in this situation—that is, they would declare that the marriage never started because the vows were taken in an invalid way, without sufficient forethought. A Catholic court would certainly annul a marriage if one of the couple felt that they were under emotional duress from their parents or if they were not sufficiently mature when they made their vows. Personally I don't like the idea of annulling a marriage. I think it's the responsibility of the minister who officiates at the wedding to make sure beforehand that the couple are properly prepared for their vows and to refuse to marry them if he thinks that they aren't.

The only biblical grounds for divorce occur when one of the four marriage vows is broken, and although some people might argue that the vow about "conjugal love" means "being in love," this is very unlikely. Equally someone might argue that the principle behind this, which I have termed "physical affection," includes showing the natural affection that only comes from being "in love." However, this would be stretching the principle too far, because no one can be required to be responsible for something that they cannot control.

Jesus discouraged divorce even when vows were clearly broken, saying that Moses did not "command" divorce but he "allowed" it when vows were broken in a "hardhearted" way, which means something like "constantly" or "unrepentantly." Marriage is not just a convenient way for two people to live together—it is a sworn agreement that two people make to each other in God's presence that they will live for each other, come what may.

Love doesn't just come from "chemistry" or from Cupid's arrow, but from human actions and reactions, from devotion and demonstrations of affection. Most marriages go through tough times when the spouses fall "out of love," but unless one of them has done something terrible, there is usually no reason this shouldn't be reversed. Arranged marriages, as in New Testament times, often start out with nothing more than one or two meetings during which the couple find that they like each other and agree to get married. Love can grow and it can regrow, if both parties are willing to help it happen.

I realize that this is not the answer you may have wished to hear, and that there will be hard times ahead, but I pray that you will be able to help your daughter and son-in-law through this difficulty in their marriage.

A SUGGESTED SOLUTION: JESUS WAS SPEAKING ONLY ABOUT BETROTHAL

> I would like to thank you for your work in regard to the issue of biblical divorce. Here in the States, many pastors refuse any type of divorce on the grounds that when Jesus was discoursing with the Pharisees, Jewish law allowed divorce only during the betrothal or one-year period before the actual marriage. When Jesus made his fornication or *porneia* exception, their claim is that he was referring to the one-year period before marriage. Essentially, they only allowed what we would in modern times call "broken engagements."

Reply: It's true that there was often a one-year betrothal in first-century Judaism and that the breaking of a betrothal required a divorce certificate. This certificate wasn't strictly necessary but was given "just in case," to provide proof that the woman was free to marry someone else. It's also true that if a person was unfaithful during the betrothal period it was considered equivalent to adultery. But, to answer your question, it is not true that divorce was allowed only during betrothal—the Pharisees allowed it at any point in marriage. And it is also not true that *porneia* (the Greek word for "sexual immorality" in Mt 19:9) only meant unfaithfulness during betrothal; it was a word with a wide meaning, including committing adultery, going to prostitutes (as in 1 Cor 6:13-18) and all other forms of sexual immorality.

For this theory to work, it would mean that Jesus used language differently from all the other Jews and Greeks of his time, so that when he used the word *porneia* he meant "unfaithfulness during betrothal" instead of just "sexual immorality" (the normal meaning of the word). If we believe that Jesus was honestly trying to communicate with his hearers (and readers), we have to assume that he meant what they would have thought he meant.

FROM A GUILTY AND REPENTANT CHURCH LEADER

I am indeed an adulterer. I was a deacon in my church and an educator in school. However, my wife and I were not a good match. Nonetheless, I stayed for twenty-six years. Tried hard to be dogmatic like her and her family. No dancing, no shorts, no public swimming, etc. Our marriage looked good on the surface. No alcohol, no abuse, no gambling, etc. Great children.

When our oldest son was killed in a car accident, I lost it. I went on the road as an entertainer and went wild. No mistake. Just plain lust, low character, etc. We divorced. I apologized publicly in two churches, re-signed as a deacon, left our church. After two years I met a lady, and we have been dating several months now. She knows all my story and the shame and guilt I bear. The brand I carry. We started going to church in my hometown. I baptized her five months ago. The church loved it. But now if we marry, the elders are going to admon-ish us and tell her she is living in adultery even though she had nothing to do with it. If we marry we will not be welcome any-more and may be asked to leave since we will be living in public sin and are going to hell. Your comments please. How do I fight this?

Reply: What a sad story. No one could fail to understand the strain you were under when your son was killed or to realize that your sin was partially caused by those circumstances.

This doesn't mean that you did not sin—and you haven't tried to deny it. You have admitted your sin before God and the church, and like all confessed and repented sins, it is now forgiven.

Although the sin is forgiven, its consequences are still there—the promises that you made to your former wife remain broken, and your children are still without their father. Paul said that in a situation like yours, that is, if you divorced without biblical grounds, you must remain unmarried while you seek reconciliation with your former partner. This means that before you remarry, you must make sure that your former wife does not want to be reconciled. You are the one who broke the marriage vows, and she, as the wronged partner, should decide if she wants a reconciliation—though of course if she has remarried, then that marriage should not be broken up.

If your former wife does not want a reconciliation, are you now free to remarry? On the basis of my research I would say yes. But as you realize, many churches do not understand the Bible in this way, and I'm afraid you are probably right to expect problems. God be with you on the difficult road ahead.

FROM A REMARRIED MAN WHOSE CHURCH WANTS HIM TO GET DIVORCED

My wife and I are both divorced. Her ex-husband is still alive; however, my ex-wife has passed away. We are very concerned about the issue of whether or not we are living in adultery, as it seems Jesus teaches. I have read some of your articles, and it appears that what is important are the *reasons* for the divorces. I know members of the Church of Christ who insist that the only way for us to escape living in adultery is to divorce one another and remain unmarried. I realize divorce is a travesty; it hurts children, parents, friends and many others. Please help us understand the truth. If we are in fact living in adultery, then I know there will never be any hope for us in serving the Lord—teaching, witnessing, or even attending our local church.

Does our divorce and remarriage put us in a class of "unforgivable" people, if we insist on remaining married? That would appear to be the case. I can't honestly see how another divorce could make things right. I understand that you may not be able to answer this, as you probably are inundated with e-mails, as most of us are. However, I need an answer. Not smooth, easy words, but the truth.

Reply: I agree that another divorce won't help, because two wrongs don't make a right. I also agree that Jesus' teaching about divorce does depend on the reason for the divorce—because he was criticizing the new groundless divorce for "Any Cause."

Was your wife's divorce based on valid biblical grounds? A biblical divorce is one that is initiated by the victim of unfaithfulness, of neglect of material support or physical affection, or of abuse. If it wasn't, then your church is right—technically you are committing adultery because your wife does not have a biblically valid divorce.

If you are committing technical adultery, Jesus did not mean that you should now divorce, any more than he expected that those who commit technical adultery by looking lustfully at someone should gouge out their eyes. When he said to "gouge out your eye" and "cut off your hand and throw it away" (Mt 5:29-30), he was using preacher's rhetoric to emphasize his point. And when Jesus said in the next verse that remarriage after an invalid divorce is technically adultery (Mt 5:31-32), he was careful not to add, "Therefore divorce her," just in case someone foolishly acted on it! Unfortunately some people did castrate themselves based on what Jesus said, and some people do teach "therefore divorce" based on something Jesus never said.

I'm glad that you want to do the "right" thing. I pray that God will guide you to the correct path.

FROM SOMEONE WHO WANTS A SERVICE OF REPENTANCE WHEN SHE MARRIES

I came across your website by chance, as if God was guiding me to your words. I have not found much consolation from the words of Christians (about remarriage).

I am a Christian and have been a single parent for six years; my children are now teenagers, and I have been divorced for five years. I have now met someone who was divorced twenty years ago. Both divorces were based on a breakdown of the marriage, and there was no third party involved. He was a Christian, but the breakdown of the marriage and subsequent divorce left him disillusioned with his Christian beliefs. So much so that one of his relations did not communicate with him for twelve years. He subsequently lived with a woman and her child for fifteen years, supporting both families although never remarrying. We have a lot of common interests, although he still turns his back on Christianity. In your paper you say that you conduct a short service of "repentance for broken promises." I have never heard of a service like this, but I feel that I would like something like that if I was ever to remarry.

However, how does this man get over the past and accept God's Word again? Our relationship is developing through plowing through arguing based on his nonacceptance of my faith. I have told him that I don't see the need to place the difference in views between us. He is knowledgeable of why Christians take Communion, so I take it that he was a practicing Christian before his divorce.

Reply: The happiness you've found seems fragile because your friend has rejected the faith that is so important to you. It might be that he has rejected the church because the church and Christians rejected him. When the question of marriage comes up, this may prompt him to reconsider his faith, and a service of repentance may be just what he needs. When he sees that Jesus loves him and forgives his broken marriage, just as he forgives other broken promises, this may give him the courage to face Christians again. I pray that God may help you in your relationship with him.

ABOUT SOME NEW CHRISTIANS WHOM THE CHURCH REFUSED TO MARRY

My wife and I were following up with a young couple in our church (the man had just trusted Christ on their first visit to our church) who were not married but were living together. Needless to say, it was a touchy situation, and we decided to focus on their spiritual growth and pray that the Holy Spirit would bring their need to change their living situation to their attention. Eventually we did speak to them about this, and they responded very well. They soon made plans to get married and decided to stop living together until this happened.

However, she called our pastor after going to our church for over six months, asking about getting married in our church and by him.... At this point some of the church's policies had to be dealt with, and our pastor and I got together and visited this couple together. At that time he handed her the church policy regarding marriage in our sanctuary and by the pastor. I watched as tears ran down her cheeks as she read this document. They almost left the church as a result of the hypocrisy in our policy, and it was only because some close relationships had developed, including that with my wife and I, that they have stayed and become very active. He now sings as part of our worship team, and she is the church secretary.

Partially due to this and similar incidents, our church has changed our policy, and we have some spelled-out conditions that are much more reasonable and have provided the opportunity to come before the elder board to talk about it. Our church policy now is that we will marry those for whom there no longer is a possibility of being reconciled to their former spouse, that is, he/she has passed away or has remarried. That still does not cover all eventualities, such as when your former spouse is "living in sin" rather than choosing to remarry. Of course the church would rather error on the side of being conservative.

I am looking forward to the completion of your book. I may not agree with all of your arguments or conclusions, but I am sure it will help me to form a better understanding of what God has to say on this topic. I may recommend it to our elder board for reading and suggest it to our pastor.

Reply: I'm really impressed by your church board, which was willing to reconsider and change its policy in the light of this incident. It's too easy to dig your heels in and say, "We've always done it this way." But I also understand those who may want to stick with the church's traditional policies (even though they are harsh and seemingly hypocritical) because they believe them to be biblical. We should always follow the Bible, even when it seems difficult. The amazing thing is that your new church policy is almost exactly what the Bible does say, according to my studies.

I pray that other churches will be like yours—ready to seek the Lord's will and ready to take into account the latest discoveries that help us understand the Bible's teaching.

FROM SOMEONE WHO ADMITS BEING JUDGMENTAL

About six months ago I discovered that the wonderful person I was dating (at that stage for one-and-a-half years) had been previously married and was divorced. I had known that he had a secret from his past, and it had taken me months to convince him that I would not judge his past, because who he was now was important. Anyway, when he told me that he was divorced, I instantly thought that I had to end the relationship (hmmm, so much for being nonjudgmental). At the time I also saw the irony in that he could have done absolutely anything else (e.g., murder) and I could be with him, just not have been divorced.

Needless to say, I did a lot of reading, and it is sites like yours that can make a difference to people's lives. So all I wanted to say was thank you!

Reply: I'm really pleased that you were able to see past your prejudice. Some church boards make the mistake that you avoided. They would happily have an ex-murderer as their pastor, and even boast about it, but they would not want a divorcee, even if he or she were the wronged partner in the marriage breakup. It's a funny world.

ABOUT A CHURCH IN WHICH SEPARATED PERSONS CANNOT BE DEACONS

The deacons and pastor at my home church (Southern Baptist) have recently decided that members who have separated from their spouses (regardless of the length of the separation or whether there are biblical grounds for divorce) cannot serve the church as deacons or on the church council.

They point to the qualification that leaders must be "good managers of their household" and that 1 Corinthians 7:10ff. specifically prohibits marital separation. They also believe that divorced members have "resolved" their marital problems and, therefore, are eligible to serve in these capacities.

Reply: This is an interesting idea, and I think it has a lot of good sense. I'm pleased to hear that your church isn't making the common mistake of interpreting "husband of one wife" (or literally "man of one woman," 1 Tim 3:2) and "wife of one husband" (or literally "woman of one man," 1 Tim 5:9) to mean "not remarried." In New Testament times those phrases meant someone who was faithful,[1] like the modern phrase "a one-woman man." Timothy was being told to make sure his deacons were not sexually immoral, which was very difficult in a society where you were allowed to sleep with your slaves and where a host was expected to provide prostitutes after a banquet.

I'm also pleased that your church is taking seriously Paul's teaching about separation, which most Christians treat far too lightly. Paul tells Christians that they should not separate, except by agreement for a short period of prayer (1 Cor 7:5). If people separate without divorcing, their partners are left in limbo and powerless. They are not able to have their old relationship, and they can't move forward to form a new relationship. That's why Paul tells those who have separated that they must seek reconciliation (1 Cor 7:11) and tells those who have been divorced by separation against their will that they are "not enslaved" (1 Cor 7:15)—they can treat the separation like a proper divorce, which frees them to get remarried. Christians often think that separation is better than divorce—the opposite of what Paul taught. So, all in all, I think your church has got it about right.

FROM MOZAMBIQUE, ABOUT POLYGAMY AND DIVORCE-BY-SEPARATION

We work in Beira, Mozambique, where marriages form by coming together and end by separation. Faithfulness is uncommon and life-long union rare. The people with whom we work are also polygamous. Our next-door neighbor has three wives and fourteen children. They frequently rely on the Old Testament to justify their way of life.

Reply: In the New Testament Jesus teaches against polygamy (which was allowed in the Old Testament and was still allowed in first-century Judaism), while Paul teaches against divorce-by-separation (which was the normal way to get divorced in Greco-Roman society) and against marital faithlessness (which was common in the Gentile world). It sounds like you are having to deal with the problems of all these New Testament societies rolled into one!

We often ignore Jesus' teaching against polygamy—because most of us in Western culture never face the issue—but it was an important part of his teaching in which he disagreed with the majority of Jews in his day. It must be exciting to see a situation where the New Testament applies so obviously, but it must also be very difficult because you face the same overwhelming task as the early Christians. I pray that God will help you as he helped them.

FROM SOMEONE WHO WANTS TO KNOW MY MOTIVES

I appreciate the work you've done, and I agree with the position you've taken.

Do you come from a broken home? Did your parent remarry? Have you been involved in a divorce? Have you been remarried?

Thank you again for your insightful work.

Reply: I'm extremely fortunate that no one in my family is divorced. My mother married my father after the death of her first husband, and my brother and two sisters and I are all once-married and remain happily married. But as a minister I met many Christians whose marriages had broken up and whose remarriages appear to have been blessed by God. It is for them that I carried out these studies and for those in destructive marriages who feel that they are not allowed to divorce. Also, I would be pleased if those who will be getting married, and those who are already married, would pay careful attention to the Bible's emphasis on marriage vows. We often take these vows too lightly.

FROM SOMEONE WHO THINKS I AM TEACHING THIS FOR MONEY

A broad path to hell and a narrow one to heaven. All the excuses for divorce and remarriage the preachers come up with to keep their money coming in. God doesn't change; men do. You can't break a covenant that both of you make to God and God seals it when you marry. The one that commits adultery and remarries is committing adultery and should get divorced. But I understand you need your income and tithe money. You know it is amazing to me, they go uptown to get married and down-town to get a divorce or to a money-hungry so-called preacher to tell them it's all right. A good preacher would say no divorce, and if you do, you have to live a single life the rest of your life because that's what you reap of your sowing.

The only way to stop an adulterous mar-riage is to get out of it. He told the woman at the well "Go and sin no more"—no more sex or men. Too bad if she has to raise her kids by herself; she reaps what she sowed. I am not trying to be hard on people, but other people reaped what they sowed in the Bible. Like Moses for getting upset and hitting a rock—sounds petty to me, but not to God. It's amazing how preachers can bend the truth and twist it to fit their wants and desires. But God said they would in the last day.

Reply: I sympathize with your criticism of preachers who teach what people want to hear in order to gain a larger income, though this is very rare. I have applied all the knowledge and intelligence the Lord has given me to studying the Bible, and I ask you to prayerfully judge what I have found out, instead of rejecting it merely because the conclusions are different from what you think the Bible says.

Although I'm not teaching these things in order to make money, I do hope that you will buy my book!

IT IS FOR YOU TO JUDGE

These e-mails demonstrate that there are a lot of people who need practical solutions, and I hope I've been able to show you that the Bible does have them. Most of the work behind these studies was conducted in the privileged academic environs of Cambridge, using the unparalleled resources of the Tyndale House library. Here I had access to a vast array of historical sources, including all the relevant ancient Jewish literature and papyri, much of which had never been examined by other scholars who worked on this subject.

My aim was not to find an easy answer but to honestly discover what the New Testament meant to its first hearers and readers. I made the wonderful discovery that the New Testament teaching is eminently practical and that it demonstrates God's continuing love for us, even after the sin of breaking marriage vows. I found that both Jesus and Paul condemn groundless divorce, but both allow the victim of broken marriage vows to divorce. I also found that divorce implies the right to remarry.

Other scholars have come to the same conclusions simply by applying common sense—though they failed to find a biblical basis for them. I was much more fortunate than they because of the unequaled access I had to historical and cultural data about the context of the New Testament.

My parting plea to you is that you do not judge other scholars harshly for what they did not know, but please do apply critical judgment to what I have said. Do not simply accept what you have read here, or simply dismiss it, but consider the evidence and pray about it. I have tried to hear what God says to us all by listening in on what he said to first-century believers, but whether or not I have succeeded is for you to judge.

STUDY GROUP BRIEFING NOTES AND DISCUSSION QUESTIONS

These discussion sessions can be used in a Bible study setting or after a presentation based on the material in this book. Each session contains three parts:

- brief notes on a Bible passage that can be used as the basis of a study

- summary of relevant sections of this book, which can be used as material for a presentation

- discussion questions

The last of the six sessions is optional because it deals with the more general topic of how we read the Bible. This issue comes up in various sections of the book and is something that many people won't have thought through. You may decide that this topic is so fundamental that, rather than leaving it to the end, the series should start with this session.

The questions are designed to provoke discussion rather than produce a straightforward answer; the leader should use them as tools to produce an exchange of ideas. There is no need to answer them in the order presented or to complete all the questions.

A group will work well if the leader and the "expert" are separate people. The "expert" should give a talk or introduce the Bible passage and be familiar with the material. The leader should direct the discussion and keep everything moving. This does not mean that the leader should be the main speaker—he or she should in fact try to be the person who says the least, because the leader's main role is to encourage and aid the debate. The "expert" should also try to keep out of the discussion except when the leader invites him or her to make a contribution.

In a group Bible study, members will best remember the things they have found out for themselves and what they have said themselves. They may *possibly* remember what the "expert" has said, and they will *probably* remember what other group members have said (especially if it was related to a story with emotional content). Therefore a successful group discussion is one in which all people feel that they have personally discovered something (thus the expert should leave some things to be discovered) and in which all people have contributed something (so the leader should make sure everyone has their say).

STUDY 1. FOUR GROUNDS FOR DIVORCE IN THE OLD TESTAMENT

Notes on Jeremiah 3:1-8

Verse 1: Israel, the northern nation, has been divorced by God for her adultery, and she wants to return. Jeremiah has doubts about this because Deuteronomy 24:1-4 says that a woman who has been divorced for her adultery and has gone off to marry someone else cannot simply divorce her second husband and return to her first.

Verses 2-3: God, through Jeremiah, reminds Israel that she has broken her marriage vows. She has taken lovers, and although God tried to warn her to repent by withholding rain, she refused to do so.

Verses 4-5: The people of Israel cried to God, calling him "Father" and asking him to stop

being angry with them. But they also continued in their sin, so they clearly weren't
genuinely repentant.

Verse 6: Jeremiah now turns to the southern
nation of Judah and its new king, Josiah, who
was one of the few good kings in the last
years of this nation. Judah is falling into the
same sin as Israel.

Verses 7-8: Jeremiah tries to use the example of the northern nation of Israel to warn
the nation of Judah. Even though Judah sees
that God has divorced Israel, she still carries
on committing the same spiritual adultery.

Summary of chapter two regarding the ground of unfaithfulness in Deuteronomy 24

The case recorded in Deuteronomy 24:1-4
concerns a woman who was divorced for
"sexual immorality" (presumably adultery,
though there are other possibilities), who
then married someone else and finally wants
to remarry her first husband. This ruling says
that she cannot, though the reason isn't
clear. Some scholars have suggested that it

is to prevent the possibility of a husband's pimping his wife to a series of different "husbands."

This case provided the basis for the law that adultery is a ground for divorce, and thereby the basis for one of the marriage vows.

Summary of chapter three regarding three more grounds for divorce in Exodus 21

Exodus 21:10-11 is part of a law code, but the details are likely to be based on another actual case where a man took a slave as his wife and then later took a second wife. He was tempted to treat the second wife as his favorite, but this ruling tells him that he cannot neglect his first wife by neglecting to give her food, clothing or physical affection. If this law applied to the least important member of society—a former slave—it is clearly a fundamental right for *every* married person.

This case provided the basis for the other three grounds for divorce and thereby the other three marriage vows.

Discussion questions

1. If you were asked to craft a law on divorce and decide the grounds on which one could get divorced, what grounds would you include? How would you word the corresponding marriage vows?

2. Moses gave all women in Israel a privilege that was given to only high-ranking women in other nations. Can you think of any extra privileges or opportunities that rich people have in our society when they are divorced? Does divorce make people better off or worse off?

3. Moses was particularly concerned for women because they suffered more than men when a marriage broke down. In what ways do men and women suffer differently in marriage breakup in our society? Who do you think suffers more? Who do you think are usually the ones who break their marriage vows—men or women?

4. Which Old Testament picture of God's relationship with Israel works best for you—a peace treaty contract or a marriage contract? Which picture best illustrates your

relationship with God? Are there other illustrations that you prefer?

5. How much do you think God's "marriage" and "divorce" were just an illustration? For example, which of the following do you think he actually experienced: love, disappointment, jealousy, anger, pain of separation or loneliness after divorce? What other feelings can a divorcee experience?

6. The prophets do not appear to hesitate to talk about God as a divorcee. Why do you think this sounds so strange—and perhaps mildly blasphemous—to many Christians? Do you think "divorcee" should be a negative label in today's society or in today's church?

STUDY 2. JESUS' TEACHING ON ADULTERY AND THE NEW "ANY CAUSE" DIVORCES

Notes on Matthew 19:3-12

Verse 3: With a clear reference to Deuteronomy 24:1, the Pharisees ask Jesus what he thinks about the new "Any Cause" divorces.

Verses 4-6: Jesus digresses—he doesn't answer the Pharisees' question but talks about marriage, saying that it should be life-long and monogamous.

Verses 7-8: The Pharisees go back to the question and ask Jesus about the divorce certificate in Deuteronomy 24:1—isn't it compulsory sometimes (that is, in cases of adultery)? Jesus says, "No, but it is *permitted,* in cases of hardheartedness."

Verse 9: Answering the question, Jesus says that Deuteronomy 24:1 does not allow divorce except for sexual immorality. He also says that divorce for "Any Cause" is invalid, so remarriage would be equivalent to adultery.

Verses 10-12: Jesus teaches that marriage isn't compulsory.

Summary of chapter five regarding Jesus' teaching

Deuteronomy 24:1 says that divorce is allowed for "a cause of sexual immorality." The Hillelites interpreted this to include divorce both for "Any Cause" and for "sexual immorality." The Shammaites' interpretation was different, saying that there is no divorce (in Deut 24:1) except for sexual immorality, and Jesus agreed with this.

Summary of chapter eight (one section): Didn't Jesus allow only one ground for divorce?

Jesus (and the Shammaites) did not mean that there were no grounds for divorce except for sexual immorality *in the whole Old Testament,* but this is the only ground in the phrase "a cause of sexual immorality" in Deuteronomy 24:1.

Discussion questions

1. Why do you think the "Any Cause" divorce was so popular in Jesus' day? If people today had the choice of proving in court that their partner was adulterous or simply getting a quiet divorce, which would they choose? Do you think Joseph was wrong to choose this type of divorce?

2. Jesus said that you can divorce someone who hardheartedly breaks his or her marriage vows, but how do you think this would work in practice? Who would decide that the person is hardhearted (stubbornly

unrepentant)—the other partner, their minister or someone else? How long would you personally put up with a partner who did not provide material support or physical affection, or who was adulterous?

3. In a few Muslim countries, adultery is a criminal offense. Should Christians campaign for this in our country? If so, what do you think the penalty should be? Do you think divorce should be compulsory for adultery?

4. Jesus agrees with the Shammaites and quotes their slogan—do you think he was secretly a Shammaite? Do you think he should have avoided quoting their slogan and used his own words? Some Christians have been labeled as Marxists in the past for using language like "economic exploitation." Can you think of other examples where Christians get labeled based on the language they use?

5. How would you advise a couple or a family who was always having arguments about the best way to survive those arguments?

STUDY 3. PAUL'S TEACHING ON THE OTHER THREE BIBLICAL GROUNDS

Notes on 1 Corinthians 7:1-15, 26-35

Verse 1: The Corinthians have written to Paul asking what he thinks about the saying "It is good not to touch a woman."

Verses 2-5: Paul says that married couples should not deprive each other because (a) they have made a vow, so they "owe" each other a "debt," and (b) prolonged abstinence leads to sexual temptation.

Verses 6-9: Some people (like Paul) have the gift of singleness.

Verses 10-11: If you are married, Paul says, you must not use the Roman divorce-by-separation by walking out or sending your partner out of your house. And if you have already done this, you should try to reverse it.

Verses 12-14: If you have an unbelieving partner who is willing to stay in the marriage, you should not initiate a divorce.

314

Verse 15: If your unbelieving partner divorces you, there is nothing you can do but accept it.

Verse 26: The "present distress" (probably a famine) makes marriage much more difficult at this time, so Paul advises people to wait if they can.

Verses 27-28: Whatever state you are in, try to avoid getting married at present. You aren't sinning if you marry, but it won't be easy.

Verses 29-31: These troubles may increase as they lead up to the end of the world!

Verses 32-35: But if you are married, don't neglect your responsibilities to give material support to your partner and "please" them with things of the world. If you aren't married, you can devote more time to serving the Lord.

Summary of chapter six regarding Roman divorce-by-separation and modern groundless divorces

Paul approves of marriage in general and emphasizes the marriage vows that promise physical affection and material support (food and clothes).

Paul says that Christians should not use the Roman groundless divorce, and he assumes that no Christian would provide grounds for divorce by breaking their marriage vows. This means that only a non-Christian would cause a divorce.

If your non-Christian partner divorces you, there is no way under Roman law to prevent this, so you should accept it.

Summary of chapter eight (second half) regarding the four Old Testament grounds for divorce in Paul

Paul regards abandonment as grounds for divorce based on neglect. The vows to feed and clothe can be generalized as material support. The vow to love can be generalized as physical affection.

Discussion questions

1. Do you know any people who have felt that they are not allowed to divorce when

common sense says that they should? Would this understanding of the biblical grounds have helped them?

2. In what ways was the Roman world like the modern Western world, and in what ways was it different?

3. The Romans thought it was immoral for people to have more than one wife but it was OK to divorce one day and get remarried the next. Which do you think is more immoral? Who are more immoral—a couple who live together faithfully without marrying, or someone who divorces and remarries four times consecutively?

4. When people want to divorce their spouse because he or she is a non-Christian, Paul says they should not (1 Cor 7:12-13). But Paul also says that they shouldn't marry non-Christians when they have the choice (1 Cor 7:39). Do you think that he is being inconsistent? Do you think it is a sin for a Christian to marry a non-Christian, or is it just unwise?

5. Paul advised the Corinthians not to get remarried during a famine because it would be hard to take care of their children. Do

you think a famine would be a reason to avoid marriage in our society? In what kinds of circumstances would you advise someone not to get married? In what circumstances would you advise someone to get married?

6.	Some Christians in Corinth thought that a celibate lifestyle was superior to a married one. Do you think this might be true for some people? How would people know if this was the right path for them? Do you think it is still true, as in Paul's day, that a single person has more time for serving the Lord?

7.	Rabbinic Jews before the time of Jesus needed to decide when people had broken their marriage vows, so they defined how much money the man had to spend on food and clothes and how much cooking and sewing the woman had to do. They even defined how often the man had to perform his conjugal duties! How can we tell when people have broken their marriage vows without making similar definitions? When would you say that someone was guilty of neglecting material needs? When would you say that someone was guilty of neglecting physical affection?

318

STUDY 4. "TILL DEATH US DO PART" AND REMARRIAGE

Notes on 1 Corinthians 7:10-15, 39-40

Verses 10-11: Paul tells those who are married not to use the Roman divorce-by-separation, and if they have done so already, then they must remain unmarried so that they can be reconciled if possible.

Verses 12-14: If you are married to an unbeliever, it is still a holy marriage, and you must not break it up.

Verse 15: If the unbeliever walks out, there is nothing you can do to save the marriage because this is legal divorce, and there is nothing you can do to bring about reconciliation because *they* have chosen to end it. Therefore you are "no longer bound"—you are free to remarry.

Verses 39-40: Widows are also free to remarry, and (contrary to the levirate law of Deut 25:5-10) Christian widows can marry whomever they want, so long as they marry a Christian.

Summary of chapter seven regarding texts that appear to deny remarriage until a former partner dies

Matthew 19:5: "One flesh" is not an irreversible oneness; otherwise anyone who visited a prostitute before conversion could not marry (compare 1 Cor 6:15-20).

Matthew 19:6: "Let no one separate" implies that one can separate but should not unless there are biblical grounds.

Matthew 19:9 seems to imply that a divorcee is still married in God's eyes, but the context is about those who have an invalid divorce based on "Any Cause" and not about those divorced on biblical grounds.

Romans 7:2 does not mention divorce, because this is not a teaching about marriage and divorce but a picture of marriage to the law and then to Christ. The law is like a very upright and correct man who would never break any marriage vows, so there would never be grounds for a divorce.

1 Corinthians 7:39-40 does not mention divorce, because it is addressing widows.

Summary of chapter nine: everyone, including Paul, assumed that divorcees could remarry

Everyone in Jewish society assumed remarriage was a right, and it was a duty if they did not have children. Everyone in Roman society regarded remarriage as a legal obligation.

Paul quietly assumes that Christians can remarry. If he had wanted to say that they could not, he would have needed to say so very clearly indeed.

Summary of chapter ten: should you get divorced if you remarry after an invalid divorce?

Redivorce would be breaking a new set of marriage vows, and two wrongs don't make a right.

Matthew 5 puts Jesus' saying about "remarriage is adultery" with other examples of preacher's rhetoric, like "anger is the same as murder" and "cut off the offending body part." Even in this section, Jesus does not tell people to divorce their new partners.

Discussion questions

1. Paul says Judaism is like being married to the law and Christianity is like being married to Christ (Rom 7:1-4). What does this imply about differences between Christianity and Judaism? Do you think that these two faiths are still different in these same ways? If not, which has changed?

2. When Romans became decadent and luxury-loving, they had far fewer children, so Augustus passed laws to encourage marriage and childbearing. Most developed countries are now in a similar situation. Do you think it is time that Christians taught "be fruitful and multiply" as a command from God?

3. If people are having trouble with their marriage, God wants to help heal the breakdowns. What kind of things should

we be praying for to help them? Is there anything else that we can do without intruding into their privacy?

4. Jesus says polygamy is not what God intended, even in the Old Testament. Does this mean that Abraham, Jacob, David and others were sinning by having extra wives? What do you think missionaries should say to converts who have more than one wife—should they tell them to divorce all but one wife? If so, who should look after the divorced wives, and should they be allowed to remarry?

5. Paul tells the person who divorced without good grounds to remain unmarried and try to become reconciled. Do you think this person is free from this command if the former partner rejects the offer of reconciliation and marries someone else? When can you be sure that the other person won't change his or her mind?

STUDY 5. WEDDING VOWS AND REMARRIAGE IN CHURCH

Notes on Ephesians 5:21-33

Verse 21: This ends the previous section with "submit to each other," then verse 22 onward looks at the details about who submits to whom, and how.

Verses 22-24: Wives submit as we all submit to Christ.
Verses 25-27: Husbands love sacrificially, like Christ.

Verses 28-29: Keep the marriage vows (to love, feed and clothe) as Christ does.

Verses 30-33: Husbands and wives become one, as we become one with Christ.

Summary of chapter eleven regarding modern marriage vows

Our marriage vows come from Exodus 21:10 via Ephesians 5:28-29 and have not changed much except that the language is a bit more formal.

The vow to obey is new—this was added in Roman times in an attempt to bring order back into society using Aristotle's philosophy. Early Christians were not entirely happy with it and taught a modified version of this morality.

When broken vows result in divorce, we should certainly allow the wronged partner to remarry in church, but what about the guilty one? Perhaps it could be permitted after a service of repentance for broken promises.

Summary of chapter fourteen (second half) regarding church practice

Similar conclusions to those in this book have been found by previous scholars, and the new evidence now makes them difficult to ignore.

These conclusions are useful in marriage counseling, but many churches are too reliant on tradition for their practices to change at this stage.

Discussion questions

1. What do you think the church should do to encourage people to get married and to discourage divorce? Should we discourage church attendance by unmarried couples or bar them from membership? If people are put off by the expense of lavish weddings, is there anything we can do about it?

2. What do you think the government should do to encourage people to get married and to discourage divorce? Should the tax system benefit married couples? Should children born to married partners be given special recognition? Should schools teach against living together without marriage?

3. In marriage vows, we promise to feed, clothe and love each other, in faithfulness. If you have taken marriage vows, were you aware of what they contained? Did you have any premarriage counseling on these vows? Do you think the vows should be different now?

4. If you are married, can you remember if you vowed to obey? If you were to

marry tomorrow, would you want to promise this to your husband or wife? What does this vow mean to you?

5. Broken vows can lead to broken marriages. Do you think that we should let the people who broke their vows remarry in church? In what way might a service of repentance for broken promises be helpful? Would you let people marry in church the lovers with whom they committed adultery?

6. Do you think that the church should change its teaching when later research reveals more about what the Bible means? Do discoveries like these make you feel uneasy or excited? Do you think the scholars have been influenced by changes in modern society? Should the church depend more on tradition and less on the Bible in order to avoid such changes?

STUDY 6 (OPTIONAL). HOW TO READ THE BIBLE, INCLUDING THE OLD TESTAMENT

Notes on Matthew 5:17-48

Verses 17-20, 48: Jesus demands a *higher* regard for the Old Testament than the Pharisees had. The following examples show that he applied Old Testament principles very widely but did not always apply the details of the Old Testament commands.

Verses 21-26: The Old Testament says murder is wrong, which implies the principle that whatever leads to murder (such as hatred) is also wrong.

Verses 27-32: The Old Testament says adultery is wrong, which implies the principle that anything that leads to adultery is also wrong, such as illicit lust or invalid divorces.

Verses 33-37: The Old Testament says it is wrong to lie to God, which implies the principle that it is wrong to lie to anyone.

Verses 38-42: The Old Testament limits revenge to the degree of your loss, which implies the principle that we should limit or even forgo revenge.

Verses 43-47: The Old Testament says love your neighbor, which implies the principle that we should love everyone, including our enemies.

Summary of chapter four regarding the Old Testament for New Testament believers

Which parts of the Old Testament apply to Christians—only the moral laws and not the ceremonial laws? only the principles and not the details? only the laws affirmed in the New Testament?

Many modern legal systems are based on the Old Testament, especially Exodus 21, where laws about divorce for neglect are found.

Summary of chapter seven's section regarding the argument from silence

Silence is very significant when it is surprising, such as when Jesus lists for the rich young ruler all of the Ten Commandments that concern people (numbers five through ten) but omits the last one—the one about coveting (Mt 19:16-22).

Silence is not significant when it is not surprising, such as when we do not hear that Adam woke from his sleep after Eve was made.

Silence is certainly not significant when the *mention* of something would be surprising, such as the two passages where death is mentioned as a way to end a marriage, but not divorce. The first (Rom 7:2) concerns Jewish believers who are married to the law, and the second (1 Cor 7:39) concerns widows; in both cases it would be inappropriate to talk about these people being divorced.

Summary of chapter ten, section regarding preacher's rhetoric

Jesus is using preacher's rhetoric when he tells people to gouge out the eyes that led them to commit adultery in their heart.

Summary of chapter twelve (second half): twentieth-century readers have to work hard

The Bible comes to us in a foreign language and from a foreign culture, so we have to learn about both of these in order to know what God told the first readers—only then can we understand what he says to us. We have books and experts to help us, so we know much more about the first century than even a second-century believer would have.

The Reformation principle of *sola Scriptura* says that what we need to know for salvation is plainly understood from Scripture, though the Reformers said that many other things were "not plain in themselves, nor clear unto … the unlearned."

Discussion questions

1. Many Old Testament laws no longer apply to Christians in the New Testament, such as the festivals, sacrifices, or the death penalty for adultery or blasphemy. How do you think we should decide whether a law still applies to us today? Does this mean we have the right to pick and choose which of God's laws we should keep?

2. Many of our modern laws are based on Old Testament principles. Are there others that you think we should follow today? For example:

    • give a second tithe for the poor every three years (Deut 14:28-29)

    • do not destroy the environment during war (Deut 20:19)

3. Many church leaders in the eighteenth and nineteenth centuries criticized the introduction of musical instruments into worship, and some still do. Do you think the fact that instruments are not mentioned in reference to worship in the New Testament church is significant in this

debate? If the New Testament doesn't say whether we should use instruments or not, how should we know what is right?

4. Jesus did not mean us to literally cut off body parts that lead us to illicit lust, but some, like Origen in the second century, interpreted Jesus' statement literally—though Origen interpreted it nonliterally in the commentary on Matthew he wrote several years after castrating himself. How can we tell when Jesus is being literal and when he is using preacher's rhetoric? Should we literally turn the other cheek (Mt 5:39) and refuse to take oaths in court (Mt 5:34-37)?

5. The church has split many times in history over doctrinal matters—the Trinity, date of Easter, authority of the pope, role of priests, tongues, status of women, eschatology and so on. Why do you think the Holy Spirit lets us get confused about these things? Why do you think that Scripture was not written more straightforwardly? Do you think there would be fewer splits or more splits if women were in charge?

6. How do you personally decide what a difficult Scripture means? For example:

• "On this rock I will build my church" (Mt 16:18). Some people (mainly Catholics) think the rock is Peter, while others (mainly Protestants) think it is the statement that Jesus has just made.

• "When perfection comes..." (1 Cor 13:10). Some people (mainly charismatics) think this is the coming of Christ, while others (mainly those who think the supernatural gifts ended in the first century) think that this is the completion of the New Testament.

NOTES

Chapter 2: A Marriage Made in Paradise

[1] The Code of Hammurabi contains laws that established order in society, for example number 233: "If a builder constructs a house and does faulty work resulting in an unsafe wall, then the builder must pay to strengthen that wall at his own expense." But when accidents are out of someone's control, they were not considered to be a crime, as in number 244: "If a citizen rents an ox or an ass and if a lion kills it while it is out in the open then there is no fine."

This set of laws even gives us the first instance of an "act of God," which modern insurance salesmen often have difficulty defining. Number 249: "If a citizen rents an ox and a member of the divine assembly strikes it with lightning and it dies, then the citizen who had rented the ox must swear in the name of a member of the divine assembly that the death of the ox was an act of God, and then there is no fine."

[2] Hammurabi Code, number 36: "If her husband has gone off to the fields, ... if she has gone to live with a(nother) husband before the five years and has also borne children, her husband upon coming back shall get her back

and her children as well because she did not respect the marriage covenant but got married."

[3] Hammurabi Code, numbers 196-99: "If a citizen blinds the eye of an official, then his eye is to be blinded. If a citizen blinds the eye ... of someone who is not a citizen, the fine is eighteen ounces of silver. If one citizen blinds the eye ... of another citizen's slave, then the fine is half the price of the slave."

[4] For example, Middle Assyrian Code, number A9: "If one citizen forces the wife of another to let him kiss her, then his lower lip is drawn along the edge of an ax blade and cut off."

[5] Middle Assyrian Code, number A45: "When a woman has been given in marriage and the enemy has captured her husband, ... she shall complete two years and then she may go to live with the husband of her choice. They shall write a tablet for her as a widow."

The right of a widow is given in Middle Assyrian Code, number A33: "she may go where she wishes." This occurs frequently in ancient Near Eastern legal documents and means "she may go to live with whomever she wishes."

Chapter 3: God the Reluctant Divorcee

[1] The phrase is *ervat debar,* where the first word means "nakedness" or "sexual immorality" and the second word is a "thing" or a multitude

of other meanings including "cause" or "reason," as in 1 Kings 9:15 or Joshua 5:4. The phrase only occurs elsewhere in Deut 23:14 with regard to modesty in the camp's toilet arrangements. The translation "a matter of sexual immorality" or "a cause of sexual immorality" fits well in the context, and according to ancient Jewish interpretations it means the woman was guilty of adultery.

[2] This follows the ESV except that "conjugal love" replaces "marital rights," which is confusing here because "food" and "clothing" can also said to be "marital rights."

[3] The ESV and other recent translations speak about "the man who hates and divorces" so that God is not the one who "hates" anything. This is undoubtedly a better translation, but it is still true that this passage shows God's extreme dislike of divorce.

Chapter 5: Divorce on Demand?

[1] As noted before, the ESV actually reads "some indecency," which is translated here as "a cause of sexual immorality" because it is somewhat more literal and it fits with the terminology used throughout this book.

[2] In my academic work I have translated this as "the 'Any Matter' divorce" because this helps to convey the overlap between the Hebrew *debar* and the *Greek aitian.* The

translation "Any Cause" leans more toward the Greek than the Hebrew.

[3] This is found in *Sifré Deuteronomy* 269; Jerusalem Talmud *Sota* 1.2, 16b; and Mishna *Gittin* 9.10. The Greek of Matthew 19:9 ("whoever divorces his wife except for sexual immorality") is almost exactly the same, because both Jesus and Shammai use the typically Jewish expression "not if" to mean "except," and both use a vague general word for "sexual immorality" rather than a specific word meaning "adultery." The version in Mishna *Gittin* 9.10 is different only by one word: it says "except he has found 'a matter of sexual immorality,'" which is exactly like the different version of Jesus' saying in Matthew 5:32: "everyone who divorces his wife, except for 'a matter of sexual immorality.'" The word "matter" in Matthew 5:32 (Greek *logos*) has the same range of meaning as "matter" in Shammai's saying that quotes Deuteronomy 24:1 (Hebrew *debar,* "a word" or "a thing"). I cannot think of any way Shammai's phrase could be translated more accurately into Greek than in these words of Jesus.

[4] Philo used it in *Special Laws* 3.30: "Another commandment is that if a woman after parting from her husband for 'any cause'..." Josephus used it in *Antiquities of the Jews*

4.253: "He who desires to be divorced from the wife who is living with him for 'any cause' (and with mortals many such may arise), must certify in writing..." In the rabbinic commentary *Sifré Deuteronomy* 269 the Hillelites say that a man can divorce a woman "even if she spoiled his dinner, since it says '[any] cause,'" and then they go on to defend their conclusion that Deuteronomy 24:1 speaks both about "she who is divorced for 'a cause'" and "she who is divorced for 'sexual immorality.'"

[5] In English this sounds like "your hardheartedness" refers to the person who is divorcing, but the "you" and "your" are both plural. Therefore, Jesus is saying, "because of hardheartedness, which is found in some of you, Moses allowed some of you to divorce. Jesus does this without implying that the two groups of people are the same individuals."

Chapter 6: When Your Partner Walks Out

[1] The ESV translates "dismiss" as "divorce," which is accurate, but it might suggest that "separate" does not also imply "divorce."

[2] A more literal translation of "separates" is possible, but it would be much more clumsy. As discussed previously in this

chapter, the verb *separate* is reflexive, so it should be translated "separate himself," but the Greek could mean male or female (as the context confirms when Paul calls the partner "brother or sister"). So a literal translation would be "If the unbeliever separates themself, let them separate themself." The translation "not enslaved" in the ESV is a very good literal translation, though most versions have something less strong like "not bound." We will see in chapter nine that "not enslaved" is appropriate because it is referring back to the context of Exodus 21:10, which concerns slavery.

[3] As before, in the ESV "divorce" has been translated more literally as "dismiss."

Chapter 7: Till Death Us Do Part?

[1] Some of the early church fathers actually thought that this silence was significant. Clement of Alexandria in the second century said that "Jesus ate and drank in a special manner without giving forth the food again" (*Miscellanies* 3.7.59).

Chapter 8: Four Biblical Grounds for Divorce

[1] Origen *Matthew* 2.14.24.

[2] As we saw in chapter five, all these subjects are dealt with in Matthew 19:3-12 and some of them in Mark 10:2-12.

[3] Literally "for a man to divorce his wife."

[4] See Jerusalem Talmud *Sota* 1.2, 16b. This misunderstanding is expressed by R. Yose b. Zabida and his son R. Eleazar soon after A.D.300.

[5] As before, "marital rights" in the ESV has been changed to a more literal "conjugal rights" because food and clothing can equally be called "marital rights" in this context.

[6] Examples are listed in Mishna *Ketubot* 7.2-5.

Chapter 9: Can I Get Married Again?

[1] A copy of the *Damascus Document* was actually discovered fifty years before the Dead Sea Scrolls in the late 1890s as part of the Geniza collection, which is described in chapter eleven.

Chapter 11: Promises, Promises

[1] The ESV has a slightly more accurate but more archaic way of putting this: "Slaves are to be submissive to their own masters in everything ... so that in everything they may adorn the doctrine of God our Savior."

Chapter 12: The Teaching That Time Forgot

[1] We saw in chapter eight that even some rabbis misunderstood the Shammaite slogan just a couple of centuries later.

[2] This is a literal translation. Modern versions often try to retain the anatomical references by misleadingly translating it "heart and mind."

Chapter 13: Conspiracy?

[1] Tertullian *Wife* I.7. This was written before he joined the ascetic sect of the Montanists, so this was his viewpoint while he was still a church leader in mainstream Christianity.

[2] Alford said, "This was a question of dispute between the rival Rabbinical schools of Hillel and Shammai; the former asserting the right of arbitrary divorce, from Deut. 24.1, the other denying it except in cases of adultery." He also quoted the use of the phrase "Any Cause" in Josephus *Antiquities* 4.253.

Chapter 15: Dear Pastor...

[1] The Greek *monandros* or its Latin equivalent *univera* is common on funeral inscriptions in praise of someone who was faithful to her husband. See references in Craig Keener, ... *And Marries Another* (Peabody, Mass.: Hendrickson, 1991), pp.92-93.

For further material, questions and answers, see
www.Divorce-Remarriage.com

BACK COVER MATERIAL

Will God allow me to divorce my abusive husband?
Would it be a sin if I remarried?

Divorce and remarriage are major pastoral issues facing every church. Yet when we turn to Scripture for guidance, we often hear conflicting messages about its teachings.

David Instone-Brewer shows how, when properly understood, the New Testament provides faithful, realistic and wise guidance for the church today.

***

"David Instone-Brewer is one of today's foremost scholars on first-century Judaism and its bearing on the New Testament. In this book he blends his academic expertise with pastoral concern; he sorts through most of the toughest issues with both intellectual rigor and Christian compassion. His persuasive work on this subject has already had far-reaching influence."

CRAIG S. KEENER, Professor of New Testament, Palmer Theological Seminary, Eastern University

344

"This book offers pastors, counselors and laypersons a coherent biblical understanding of divorce and remarriage.... Discerning readers will appreciate the wealth of evidence that allows them to reach their own conclusions, while those interested in 'the bottom line' will find the author's summary principles on divorce and remarriage most helpful. A summary chapter gives helpful suggestions and questions especially useful for small group discussions. I look forward to using this most excellent book in my D.Min. family ministry class."

JACK BALSWICK, Professor of Sociology and Family Development, Fuller Theological Seminary

"This is definitely the best and most compelling work I have read on ... divorce and remarriage. Dr. Instone-Brewer marshals evidence from rabbinic literature, the Dead Sea Scrolls and other ancient texts to demonstrate the conclusion that the Bible permits ... divorce on the grounds of adultery ... neglect or abuse.... I highly recommend this work."

KENNETH L. BARKER, former secretary of the NIV Committee for Bible Translation

With fresh insights from ancient sources, Dr. David Instone-Brewer takes a deep yet engaging look at this timely topic. He writes with a scholar's mind and a pastor's heart. Clergy, counselors and church councils should read this book and then thoughtfully reflect upon his conclusions regarding a biblical perspective on divorce and remarriage. People who are thinking about marriage, divorce and remarriage should also read this book as it offers both hope and challenge."

VIRGINIA TODD HOLEMAN, Professor of Counseling, Asbury Theological Seminary

"David Instone-Brewer knows the Scriptures, and the textual and cultural background to the Scriptures, as well as any biblical scholar in the world today. He combines this scholarship with a pastor's heart for people and a commitment to the church.... Divorce and Remarriage in the Church *will become an indispensable resource for both scholars and pastors in years to come, and has the promise of reforming church practices in thousands of congregations."*

DAVID P. GUSHEE, University Fellow and Graves Professor of Moral Philosophy, Union University

***

The Rev. Dr. David Instone-Brewer is a research fellow at Tyndale House, a research library in biblical studies located in Cambridge, England. He previously served as a Baptist minister. His previous publications include *Techniques and Assumptions in Jewish Exegesis Before 70C.E., Divorce and Remarriage in the Bible and Traditions of the Rabbis from the Era of the New Testament.*

Books For ALL Kinds of Readers

At ReadHowYouWant we understand that one size does not fit all types of readers. Our innovative, patent pending technology allows us to design new formats to make reading easier and more enjoyable for you. This helps improve your speed of reading and your comprehension. Our EasyRead printed books have been optimized to improve word recognition, ease eye tracking by adjusting word and line spacing as well as minimizing hyphenation. Our EasyRead SuperLarge editions have been developed to make reading easier and more accessible for vision-impaired readers. We offer Braille and DAISY formats of our books and all popular E-Book formats.

We are continually introducing new formats based upon research and reader preferences. Visit our web-site to see all of our formats and learn how you can Personalize our books for yourself or as gifts. Sign up to Become A RHYW Registered Reader.

www.readhowyouwant.com